BILLY MITCHELL

BILLY MITCHELL

FOUNDER OF OUR AIR FORCE AND PROPHET WITHOUT HONOR

BY

EMILE GAUVREAU AND LESTER COHEN

Billy Mitchell: Founder of Our Air Force and Prophet Without Honor by Emile Gauvreau and Lester Cohen. First published in 1942

Annotated edition with footnotes and images published 2019 by The War Vault.

FIRST PRINTING, 2019.

ISBN: 978-0-359-57507-7.

CONTENTS

1 – INTRODUCTION: BLACKOUT AT LITTLE VENICE

ON AN EVENING IN JUNE 1942, two men sat at a table in a corner of a little Italian restaurant in West Thirteenth Street, New York. One of them, formerly a well-known newspaperman, since then an official investigator for the Committee on Patents of the House of Representatives, was Emile Gauvreau, co-author of this book. The other, a rugged, ageless, solid-looking man with a lined, patient face, sparse gray hair and searching brown eyes was James V. Martin [James Vernon Martin, 1885-1956], the aircraft inventor, once an officer in the Merchant Marine, and later the father of half the basic patents for things that fly.

This was a special occasion. Recently a parade had been held to welcome to New York a handful of the Allied Nations' flying heroes, including young Donald Mason, [VC-82 pilot Chief Aviation Machinist's Mate, later Ensign, later Lieutenant Donald "Don" Francis Mason] whose report, "Sighted Sub Sank Same," [Mason's famously succinct message sent to his skipper after sinking U-503 near the Grand Banks of Newfoundland] has already become a classic of the war. Tonight, there was to be a practice blackout, when the great electric-lighted city with its "white way" and sky-signs would become merely a spot of blacker darkness.

The two men sat at a special table, too, the table at which the late General "Billy" Mitchell [William Lendrum Mitchell, 1879-1936] used to dine, for the Little Venice had been his favorite restaurant. At this very table, seven and eight years before, he had night after night gathered a circle of friends about him and spoken to them urgently of the future and what must inevitably happen to America—war with Japan; the invasion of Alaska; the seizure of the Philippines—unless the heads of the Army and Navy awoke to the meaning of air-power and to what was going on in Japan and Germany.

Both the inventor and the investigator had been intimately associated with Mitchell, the gallant crusader, during the years that saw the General's desperate, single-minded, and almost single-handed, fight to awaken his sleeping countrymen to the peril which he foresaw so plainly, and which has since his death come so inevitably upon us and the rest of the world.

James V. Martin's fate, indeed, though not so dramatic or so tragic as General Mitchell's, was linked with it in disaster. Originator and owner of at least twenty-five basic devices, which are incorporated in all modern airplanes, Mitchell had seen his inventions taken from him by the Air Trust under the cover of government control, and had then been ruined and persecuted because of his refusal to manufacture the dangerous and inefficient DH [de Haviland] planes, known to the aviators who flew them (and were burned to death in them) as "flaming coffins."

While Martin sat, quickly puffing on his blackened briar pipe and listening to his companion, while Leo, the head waiter, dialing for music, tuned in on a raucous radio voice which announced, "...making over 300 ships sunk in the Atlantic since Pearl Harbor."

"Turn it off, for God's sake, Leo," Martin broke in. "I hate to think of those poor devils. Here I am, an old sailor, and I can't help them!"

Leo switched the radio into silence and came for their order.

"I see you're back in General Billy Mitchell's corner," said Leo. "Everything he told us right here has come true; battleships sunk by air bombs, big cities like Cologne destroyed from the air, France gone, the Philippines gone, just as he said seven years ago, sitting right at this table."

Vannini, the proprietor of Little Venice, came over from his bar to shake hands with the two well-remembered guests.

"Well," he greeted them, "here you are again, sitting at General Mitchell's table, and a blackout coming in a few minutes. I've just been talking to the chef, and telling him he and all his help will have to sit in the dark, with all the food cooking, and he said, 'If they'd only made General Mitchell air-boss down in Washington, we'd have plenty of light. There wouldn't have been any need for a blackout.'"

Even as he spoke, waiters began reluctantly clicking out the lights. One by one the diners stopped talking to listen, and became shadows. Even in the kitchen the clatter of pans and crockery subsided. The waiters stood about the diners' tables uncertainly, silhouettes in the gloom.

At General Mitchell's table, meanwhile, in a blackness lighted only by the occasional flare of a match applied to a pipe or a cigarette, his two friends spoke together in subdued voices about their dead hero, recalling the early days of aviation, the General's inspired conviction that the future of America's defense lay in the air, his uncannily accurate prophecies, his unconquerable determination to bring the truth to the American people, and, finally, the Gethsemane through which he passed in his defeat.

And so it happened, by the irony of fate, that there, in the dark of the blackout, which would never have been necessary if Billy

Mitchell had been listened to, was born this book which tells the story of his crusade.

It is an inspiring story, the story of a man with a vision, who, almost alone, set himself to fight the forces of bureaucratic inertia, of the pompous self-satisfied ignorance of officialdom, and, worst and most dangerous of all, the sinister predatory greed of international Big Business.

Like many another dauntless pioneer of human thought, Mitchell was laughed at, flouted, disgraced and... killed; but his ideas are marching on, his spirit is with us, his crusade is at last coming home to the hearts and minds of his countrymen, and day by day a brighter radiance shines upon his name.

2 - The Creator of the Blitz

THIS BLACKOUT, James Martin said, groping for a saucer to knock out the glowing ashes of his pipe, *this blackout seems to bring everything back. I feel like talking about him in this darkness. It has come upon us because we denied him. He was trying to pull us out into the light. It's like unrolling a scroll of prophecy to read what he said...*

He had the brave, violent nature that has always made history. The instrument he gave his life to, he knew would be used to kill, but he wanted us to have more of them than any other nation in order to save ourselves.

He knew the plane when it was nothing but an engine in a kite. But it was a new thing. That's what interested him. Billy Mitchell was a great American because he never forgot that the United States was 'a new thing' when it was invented. This country is a great invention, a history of inventions, and the blood of inventors has been its seed.

The imaginative are always laughed at and persecuted if they can see things that other people can't see. Most of us who have a great faith in something new think we could be martyrs for it, but when we come to act... well, that's a different story. Billy Mitchell devoted his life to an idea because he knew it was right. He might as well have died in flames and tortures for his belief. And he was done to death in this country, the Nation of Inventions.

I can go pretty far back about Billy Mitchell. I can't help believing after my experience with him that all things are ordained by fate. Men with a passionate belief in the same thing are bound to meet. He was born under the star that makes people 'firsts.' These people attract other people.

When he was in a hut in Alaska, working out the problem of stringing telegraph wire down the Yukon for 3,000 miles to Prince William Sound, I was a navigator taking some of the biggest ships up to the Arctic that ever went up there. While I was piloting ships through the Bering Strait and the approaches to the Aleutian Islands I was thinking of airplanes. I had a feeling that they would finally make ships go stale. I was young and I didn't want to be stuck with a has-been proposition; and while I was thinking of airplanes, off

Alaska, looking at the sky at night, Billy Mitchell was in Alaska, working on kites and thinking about the same thing.

Way up there, where the air is clean and cold, maybe thoughts meet. Vital thoughts meet anyhow. I feel sure. Well I quit the sea and met Augustus Herring [Aviation pioneer and partner of the storied Herring-Curtiss airplane company, Augustus Moore Herring, 1867-1926]. He taught the Wright Brothers the use of current surfaces, which give us the characteristics of lift and enable the airplane to fly. He was to die practically in my arms [Herring was later paralyzed by a series of strokes] of starvation, but that's another story. I remember one day when he told me, 'Well, Jimmie, I guess I've taught you all I know. From now on you're on your own.'

I'll admit I was a bit disheartened when Sam Langley [Samuel Pierpont Langley, 1834-1906] cracked up after the government had given him $50,000 to prove that he could [indeed] fly [but only get off the ground, not sustain flight]. It broke his heart, really. But it was only nine days later that the Wright brothers got off the ground at Kitty Hawk [for the first sustained flight, December 17, 1903]. I was so excited about it I couldn't sleep. I didn't think the papers had paid enough attention to it. There were a few little items about it days after it had happened.

And there was another fellow who couldn't sleep as the result of the first mechanical flight, and that was Billy Mitchell. He got Orville Wright to teach him how to fly. He was a captain in the Signal Corps then, and he made so much noise about flying machines that when the first few military planes were developed, they were turned over to him because the Army knew nothing about them. He continued to whoop it up until Congress appropriated $13,000,000 for the organization of the First Aero Squadron. That's how Billy Mitchell came to be the father of our Air Force!

Well, by that time I had found a barn on Long Island where I could begin to work out some of my own notions, a new kind of wing, the tractor biplane, ring cowling for air-cooled motors. That sort of thing. I was one of the aircraft pioneers. There were a number of us. We read every book that had been written about flying. I guess I must have fathered about fifty inventions. We went through some tough times trying to make both ends meet, but we were learning.

We had no established principles of design for flying machines. The barn was the hangar, the barnyard the runway and we had to be our own test pilots. There were no aircraft factories. If we spilled and cracked our ribs, we taped them up, and if we cracked an airplane wing, we taped that up, too. About every week, I guess, I ran down to Washington to file a new patent. Most people thought such ideas were of no value and called our machines 'fool killers.'

Then I read that Billy Mitchell had been put in charge of military planes. The idea came to me that if I could construct a plane that could carry a couple of bombs, that would be a military plane. In other words, I had an idea for a bomber, way back then. I kept designing the thing. Obviously, bombs would increase weight, which would cut down speed, but finally I thought I had it. Then began my peregrinations through the halls of Washington.

Nobody cared much about my notions. Flying patents were a dime a dozen. I interviewed clerks and cavalrymen and Indian fighters, until finally somebody let me get to Mitchell. I wonder why it was that I had to put up a fight to reach his door? Why is it always this way in Washington when an inventor goes down there with an idea?

But when they finally let me in to see Mitchell, I knew I had found my man. You didn't have to beat around the bush with him. His eyes would snap when you mentioned something new. He knew right off that I was a man of the sea, that I had paced decks, been through storms. Perhaps he sensed the storms we were to face together. He was an important man, a snappy looking captain, a distinguished graduate of the Army School of the Line, graduate of the Staff College, instructor in the Staff College. Some people had told me: 'If you can see him, you'll get somewhere. He's going to be a member of the General Staff.'

He was rubbing his joints from a crack-up down the Potomac when they let me in his office. He was laughing about it, a bit ruefully. After office hours he was perfecting his flying. I liked him at once because he admitted freely that he had made a miscalculation in landing.

People saw him crash, and laughed, he said, and it made him feel like a goddamned fool. He didn't blame it on the plane, which god knows, in those days, could have been blamed for everything. He said he had learned the greatest lesson of his life by taking a header. I told him about my own flops, and we were friends in two minutes.

'What have you got up your sleeve, Jim?' he asked me. He called me Jim just like that.

And I said: 'Captain, I think I've got a military plane. I think I've invented something that can drop bombs.'

His lean face grew taut and his eyes seemed to eat up every line on my blueprints which showed where the bombs could be suspended right under the pilot and released by some sort of a faucet arrangement. A pretty crude thing, I'll admit. I had the faucet in my pocket to show him how it worked.

'Do you get the idea, Captain?' I asked him.

He looked up at me with those eyes that seemed to burn through your skull.

'Jim,' he said, with that queer twist of his mouth, 'I'm way ahead of you!'

I felt right off that this man ought to be a general, a general of the skies; he understood, he got the feel and gist of the air, its limitlessness, its own world. His sea-gray eyes were shot with repressed eagerness when he looked at me.

I remember it was getting dark. He looked out the window at the lights coming up in the street and he turned about, with that quick, restless movement after he had thought something out.

'Listen,' he said, 'we've got things to talk about. Do you eat?'

'Not a helluva lot these days,' I said, and he burst into a laugh and clapped me on the back.

'Come on,' he said, 'let's go to dinner,' and that's how I happened to tell him about all of my inventions.

I had an idea for a flying boat, and he stopped eating while I described it. I was talking through mouthfuls because I was hungry. That was the best dinner I had ever had up to that time. You know how inventors live. But let's not go into that.

'You mean an amphibian?' Mitchell asked.

'Yes, exactly,' I said. 'I got the idea up in Alaska on my last trip. Something might happen up there someday, and we might save the territory with armed flying-boats.'

'Say!' he exclaimed, 'Say, what do you know about Alaska?' and I told him.

He was in such a state of excitement that he pushed his dinner aside. His eyes gleamed.

'While you were prowling about on your boat,' he said, 'I was up there too. We were thinking about the same thing, both of us. Why!' his enthusiasm shone in his face. 'Do you know what I did up there? I invented a tandem kite that took me off the ground. That's how I came to fly! Go ahead,' he said, 'keep talking. We're sitting on the same cloud. My God! Equal understanding. Have I been looking for that!'

Well, you know the kind of evening. Once in a lifetime, you meet a person like that, and he takes you off the earth. When I got back to my hotel, I had to wake up the clerk to take me up in the elevator. That's how late it was. And I sat on the bed, just thinking.

Mitchell told me to bring my friends down to Washington. All inventors, they were. He thought it was his duty to see men like that, to become familiar with what they were doing, to recommend the adoption of their achievements. Billy actually got some of my stuff into the War Department for consideration.

By this time, I was making money in air exhibitions and somehow, with my friends, we got my first factory going, down in Garden City, Long Island. I picked the spot because the first airfield in the country was located there.

When the winter of 1915 came around, and you know what was ahead of us then, I knew what was going to happen before a lot of people did, because Billy Mitchell telegraphed me to come down to Washington in a hell of a hurry. He told me to get all the backing I could and expand my factory. He said we were going to be pulled into the war before it was over. That's how far ahead the man could see things.

'We'll need planes,' he said. 'Do you know how many planes we've got now? Thirty-five in the whole damned Army. We've got to get busy. And I want somebody I can trust to help me get them out!'

It took me some time to get the backing. Two years went by, and while I was turning out some machines of a type which had been approved by the First Aero Squadron, Billy wired me again. I used to see him quite regularly. This time the message gave me a jolt and I went down to Washington hell-bent. I had to drive through a snowstorm to get to him; it was long before the Spring of 1917. Mitchell was pacing his office in a major's uniform.

'I've tried to keep you posted,' he said, 'because your services are going to be of infinite value to our government. We're going to need planes, Jimmy,' and he drew me into a corner of his office, 'we're going to war, but you've got to keep this news locked up in your chest. We'll need you. I'm leaving in a few days, secretly, for Europe. I'm supposed to be going on leave to Spain.

Those people who say that Woodrow Wilson first shakes his fist at Germany and then only shakes his finger afterwards are going to be knocked out of their beds. He sent for a number of us last week to find out how many planes we had. I told him. Do you know how many planes we have now in our whole fighting force?'

'About five hundred, anyhow,' I guessed.

'Five hundred, hell,' he laughed grimly. 'We've got exactly fifty-five planes. Two aviation fields and fifty-five serviceable planes. The National Advisory Committee on Aeronautics has advised the President that fifty-one of them are obsolete and the other four obsolescent That's what we've got to start with. The President is going to call for five hundred million dollars at least to build planes. This is your opportunity. I know what you can do. Get busy. I'll see some people for you. We won't be able to turn planes out fast enough. I'll keep in touch with you by cable. I'm going to run the air show over there or I'll miss my guess. Goodbye and good luck.'

As a newspaperman, you know what happened after that. The most horrible scandal in our history. If it had happened in any other country at war, the responsible parties would have been lined up and shot.

We appropriated $1,650,000,000 for aircraft and all Billy Mitchell got out of it as commander of our air forces in France was 196 planes. I don't have to tell you anything about that. I remember your headlines during the first investigation.

But Mitchell, in France, begging for planes, knew nothing about it.

Papers reaching him said the sky would be filled with planes. I remember a headline quoting Brigadier General George O. Squier, chief signal officer of the Army:

BLOW TO BE STRUCK AT GERMAN WAR MACHINE WITH 100,000 PLANES

The poor, ignorant fool. All this while the money was being squandered. Even [legendary World War I veteran, General of the Armies John Joseph] Pershing, who was no airman, God knows, was cabling his protests.

But Mitchell got planes. We had to buy them from the British and the French, 1,300 machines to fight their battles.

With what was left of his 196 machines Mitchell led the strongest aviation force ever assembled up to that time; about 1,400 planes. It was his idea. And if the truth is ever told, that broke Germany's back. That started the 'push.'

You can imagine him over there, brooding about planes. He told me about it when he got back: going down to the docks at Bordeaux, watching ships unloading, soldiers coming off, horses, mules, cannon, caissons, but no planes. Stevedores in blue denim, sweating under their load, Red Cross nurses coming down the plank, ambulances lowered by cranes, more mules, but no planes.

And finally, a year after he had been expecting them, those 196 machines arrived in a heartbreaking trickle; two, three, or six at a time and when they were put together, you know what they were: *flaming coffins!*

That's how I got into the picture. I had the facilities to make planes then. Good ones. But that $1,650,000,000 had been raked in by a monopoly made up mostly of automobile manufacturers and smart politicians. They'd grabbed an old English plane design known as the De Haviland 4, with the tank right in back of the pilot. They could make them cheap.

Our men were killed on the training fields by the dozens every week. In France, all the Germans had to do was to shoot into the gas tank and our pilots were burned alive before the machines crashed. The monopoly wanted me to make those terrible things. I knew what they were, and I turned a $10,000,000 job down.

But Mitchell had to take those 'flaming coffins' and order his men up in them. He flew them himself. He was the first American officer to fly over the battle lines. Do you remember the last time he was here he was talking about Noyon?

That's where his men were turned into flying torches for the first time and where he decided to do the air reconnoitering work himself. He was made a colonel for that.

Then came the Allied crisis. You won't find this in any history books of the first World War. The French Army was breaking up. French soldiers, tired out, had become skeptical. They were wondering why certain industrial plants in France were never bombed by the Germans and why certain German industrial plants were never bombed by the French.

Mutiny and rebellion developed in the French trenches, and in some regiments, officers had to shoot one man out of every ten. 'Disciplinary shootings,' they were called. That's why the war had to be ended. The Germans knew there was going to be a desperate drive and they brought up great concentrations of aircraft, the best of its day.

That's how Mitchell got his 1,300 planes from the Allies. It was his own strategy. General Pétain himself turned over to him a French air division of 600 planes. The Italians had 200, or about that. General Trenchard of the British was glad to serve under Mitchell. He came through with 700 planes. By that time our own planes amounted to almost nothing.

Now the whole thing was up to Mitchell. That's how he became slated for brigadier general. By this time his flights had captured public imagination. You remember the headlines:

SOLO FLIGHT HELPS END WAR

But behind all this was Mitchell, the strategist extraordinary.

St. Mihiel was an armed German peninsula cutting into the American lines. Mitchell decided to hit it from both sides. He arranged his aviation in a V about the salient. When one branch of the V smashed at the salient, absorbing the enemy fire, he let go at the rear of the enemy with the other side of the V. The salient was wiped out in the first example of mass air strategy in history.

At Chateau Thierry, Mitchell used to say, he was greatly outnumbered. The Germans would make a feint at him, first in one direction, then from the other. They wanted him to spread his air force out in all directions, in order that they might nip it off, piece by piece. He called in his bombardment planes from all sectors and concentrated them at the German center at Fère-en-Tardenois. That was an important place for the Germans. He knew, if he kept raining enough hell on it, they would have to bring up nearly all of their pursuit groups.

And that was precisely what happened. He threw his pursuit aviation at theirs. This accomplished three decisive results.

It lightened German air pressure on American ground troops, it afforded American observation the opportunity to go aloft. And vastly more important, by pitting pursuit against pursuit, and with good fighting, Mitchell began to achieve a numerical balance: the Germans no longer had superiority in the air.

Study the Argonne from the point of view of military aviation.

A great concentration of troops and troop trains behind the American lines. Some of these trains didn't move for thirteen hours.

The Germans knew about the jam and brought up attack aviation. Pershing knew that if they could strike from the air the American Army would be in a critical position. He knew because Mitchell had told him. It was an air problem that Mitchell reveled in. He sat up all night figuring it out.

Early on the next morning he struck first, blasting German centers of concentration, Romagne, Grandpré. The Germans, he figured, would throw everything they had into these sectors to defend them. Otherwise their ground forces would be compromised. And that's what the Germans did.

Again, pursuit pinched off pursuit, Mitchell's forces now gaining a numerical advantage. As this advantage became greater, Mitchell could use more planes against retreating German columns, motor trains, railroad concentrations and military emplacements.

This was what we now know as blitzing. Mitchell had created it. With complete mastery of the air, our flying forces could screen the movements of the ground forces. At last, as Mitchell often said, he knew exactly what the enemy was doing. He let fly with everything he had.

The ground troops followed up. And our Army went ahead, blasting its way into the German lines. The air decision had given our forces complete initiative. The war was practically over.

Reluctantly, now, we're beginning to admit all this in our period of slow transition from ground and sea war to the War of the Air. It may sound of course, as though Billy Mitchell won the last war. That is exactly what I think he did. He was the Napoleon of the Air. He believed in the air-blitz because he believed what his eyes could see.

And what we couldn't see, as time went on, the Germans did see. Our generals could not believe in it, because they could not believe what their own eyes had seen. That will be the verdict of history, and in a way the kindest thing that can be said.

If they did see it, if they did understand it, then why were they caught off base, why did they attempt to minimize the importance of air power? And, so, in essence, usher in the Second World War? Someday after this war is over, and it will be won by those with the greatest air power, Mitchell's importance in military history will be recognized.

We insisted on minimizing what was done in the air in our World War histories. We remembered individual flyers, great heroes like Eddie Rickenbacker, Jim McConnell, Elliott Cowdin, Lieut. William Thaw, Raoul Lufberry, and all the German planes they shot down, but we closed our eyes to the 'Air Blitz' we had invented.

We returned to our drill parades, our tactics of trench fighting and let the Germans take over everything we had shown them in the first great air battles in history, and in which we licked them.

We never studied the World War from the air viewpoint. That's why our side is taking an awful pasting at the present time.

As I have said already, all this may sound as though Mitchell won the war single-handed. Well, suppose he had been unable to get the mastery of the air over the Germans. Our own planes were useless. The German planes were getting better week by week. But Mitchell developed a new kind of war, and ancient warfare curled up forever when he finally got his planes.

What he wrote in the sky will remain. What others did under him on the ground will seem of less and less importance as the years go on—until it is almost forgotten. The fact that we crucified the greatest military prophet we ever had ought to teach us an awful lesson! But, sometimes, I wonder!

3 - "FLAMING COFFINS" AND BATTLESHIPS

HIS FRIENDS WERE STRUCK BY A MARKED CHANGE that had come over General Billy Mitchell when he returned from France in 1919. It was not a new haste, a greater impatience, but the quality of being centered on an overpowering idea. It had added a new firmness to him; that rare something which enables a man to regard difficulties but as evils to be surmounted.

Perhaps he already foresaw that the years ahead in his path were to be strewn with obstacles to divert his course, that his conclusions, his strongest convictions would be constantly exposed to ingenious ridicule. He had discovered a great truth, but it had made no impression on the Allied air leaders with whom he had conferred in France and England after the armistice. He was determined to make America understand it. Years later he was to put it into a book which was not to be appreciated until a quarter of a century after its publication, and by a horror-stricken, rocking world. His truth was a gospel he was to repeat until his last breath:

"If a nation ambitious for universal conquest gets off to a flying start in a war of the future it may be able to control the whole world more easily than a nation has controlled a continent in the past."

But the decorations he had received from President Wilson, the British, the French, the Italians, the citations from General Pershing, all the medals, "enough to sink a cruiser," as he put it, had not been presented to him as the greatest military prophet since the Battle of Formigny where the Constable of France, de Richemont, gained an impossible victory over the English in 1450, but as a daring flyer leading other heroic flyers staking their lives on an untried instrument. Only two nations in the world, Germany and Japan, were to recognize the fact that Mitchell's air strategy had revolutionized modern warfare; two nations which were to pounce upon his ideas and use them in a leap for world conquest while his own country laughed. He knew already, and determined to tell the people, what was later to be accepted as a fact and so well expressed by the scientist Roger Burlingame in his *Engines of Democracy:*

"Almost the entire ancient art of warfare has been upset by aeronautics. Secret passing of troops has become impossible except when observation planes can be annihilated. Since the arrival of the air arm the new technique of camouflage has become a necessity. New tricks

of propaganda from the air have aided in demoralizing reserve forces and breaking civilian morale.

Machine gunners, infantrymen and spies may be landed by parachute in any part of the enemy country. Bridges, railheads, roads, communications, trenches may be destroyed without the operation of ground forces.

Troops may be 'strafed' by low-flying machine-gunners. Civilian populations must be evacuated from towns. The cost of such attacks and of the effort to disperse populations in danger of them is out of all proportion to the cost of maintaining the air arm. The result is a revision of wartime economy as well as a change in field maneuvers."

For preaching these truths twenty years ahead of their acceptance by a convulsed civilization, General Mitchell was to be put to the rack and his name besmirched. He knew what to expect the moment he demanded the reason why he had received 196 "flaming coffins" from the government appropriation of $1,650,000,000. Upon his return he had immediately been made Assistant Chief of the Army Air Service, in direct charge of the training of the aviation force of the army, and was stupefied to find on the first day at his post that he was expected to fly the same murderous DH4's.

His friend, Jimmy Martin, the inventor, who had served as consulting engineer in the Air Service after he had refused to build the "flaming coffins" was the only man to whom Mitchell could turn for the complete explanation of the mystery.

There had been an aircraft conspiracy organized by industrial promoters under the leadership of a ruthless group in Ohio, later to figure in the Harding Administration. With the permission of our War Government, all airplane patents had been seized during the National Emergency by the monopoly, ostensibly to speed production. With the new Trust in control, independent manufacturers who had refused to make the "flaming coffins" had been forced out. Forty-seven inventions had been stolen from Martin himself. All the pioneer inventors Mitchell had previously met were now out of business. The government, in its desperation for planes had trustingly opened the doors of the Patent Office to the conspirators, even to the point of signing contracts which prevented the schemers from being sued by the defrauded inventors. The staggering appropriation has disappeared, and all that had come out of it was the "flaming coffin."

Blazing with anger, Billy Mitchell set to work to expose the monopoly. President Wilson appointed Charles Evans Hughes to direct a rigid investigation of the scandal. The future Chief Justice ordered indictments and criminal prosecutions, but when the newspapers had finished publishing the damning evidence no man was brought to trial, not even indicted. The leaders of the conspiracy had temporarily run to cover, waiting their chance to reappear under a new administration.

The law permitting the Trust to appropriate inventions under immunity remained unchanged. The government now had to buy airplanes from the monopoly by direct negotiation instead of through competitive bidding. The Trust had pooled all airplane patents and gripped the American people by the throat.

The monopoly was able to sell its best products to Germany and Japan and proceed unmolested. Martin, the inventor, had discovered that two aviation companies in the Trust which controlled the aviation situation during the war had been financed in their entirety by Mitsui & Co., Japanese bankers, the fiscal agents in the United States of the Japanese Government and paymasters to the German secret service still acting in this country.

This startling disclosure appeared on the official records of the Senate Committee on Military Affairs. The Trust, all-powerful, had been sending carloads of airplanes to Japan labeled as "household furniture;" planes needed by our own airmen during the war.

The most ominous commentary on the scandal was made by Gutzon Borglum, noted sculptor and aerodynamic engineer who had been appointed personally by President Wilson to dredge it to the bottom. Said Borglum after his investigation (War Frauds, Congressional Record, April 11, 1922):

There will be no convictions for this gigantic fraud, and we will get nothing, but a political burial of a crime of which Republicans and Democrats are equally guilty. If there is a man holding a prominent official position in the United States government today who is prepared to prosecute, say, one of the biggest banks in America that fairly glutted itself on the proceeds of aeronautic engines, which in turn it used to inflate prices on unnecessary quantities of war material for our Army, if there is a man in authority at Washington who is prepared to prosecute or even mention the name of this bank publicly, I should like to know his name. I can name several men high in government confidence who will not let this institution be mentioned nor let anything be done which may embarrass it.

Will you show me one man high in political preferment today who will not make the same answer and in making it, practically say: 'To hell with America if her welfare affects "the party"?' The power to tax the people of the United States and pass its legislation is bigger game than Standard Oil, Steel or the railroads combined.

There is something profoundly rotten in this aircraft scandal business. It was conceived and carried out with such intent to defraud—it was so bad in its conception and in its building, and finally in its production—so vast was the machinery of evil—that I doubt if we shall be able to do anything in aeronautics during this present generation because of what exists, and there are not in all America five or six men of power, or position who care.

There are not two! There are not five or six public men who have the character to prosecute the Air Trust, in or out of the Army, in or out of public life, and there are none in commercial life.

I do not know any who will sacrifice his job or his chance for preferment to speak the truth. The government must completely overhaul its aeronautical salvage, discard practically all the men heretofore connected with it, and put the entire department in the hands of new people, utterly free of all connection with it during or since the war. The government is choked with material, yet is asking for more money. All I can add is that I have learned not to hold Presidents responsible for all of the government all of the time.

No man in the United States could have been more aware of the appalling magnitude of the work ahead of him than Billy Mitchell when he chucked his medals into a bureau drawer and tightened his belt.

"We'll have to conduct our own private war," he told Jimmy Martin. "We've got to tell the truth to those who have a right to know it. And if we're going to tell the truth, we've got to live it constantly. I've got a plan of campaign. It will have to be spectacular to interest the newspapers and, through the press, the people will find out what is going on. We'll have to attack those inside the government who are already subordinating the airplane to all other arms of war. After we have aroused the country, we'll be ready to demand laws to wipe out the monopoly. We'll have the public with us. The government, criminally indifferent to the need of an Air program, is already powerless to prevent the sale of American airplanes to foreign powers. Japan is the nation to watch; later Germany."

All this in 1920.

Martin, who had made twelve trips to Japan as a navigator and airplane inventor and who had missed nothing in his prowlings about the Island Empire, held the same convictions. America would have to be told, even if he were reduced to shouting the truth in the street on a soapbox.

"The plain truth can be seen by the people," the inventor insisted. "If a crooked stick is in front of you, you don't have to explain how crooked it is. You lay a straight one close beside it."

"Again, I'm way ahead of you," Mitchell replied.

"That's what I'm going to do. I've got the straight stick already and I'll lay about me."

The General and the inventor shook hands on their pact. As a result of it, for seventeen years, the forces of error and greed were to arouse the passions and prejudices of men in order to thwart the two crusaders.

Martin, whose factory still limped along, was to plod on tirelessly for redress, appeal for his stolen patents before dozens of futile Congressional investigations and carry his fight through dragging Courts of Claims to the Supreme Court of the United States, until finally, his plant closed, his whole business wiped out, he was to be penniless.

The law passed during the war emergency, and which had permitted the monopoly to plunge its hand into the grab-bag of airplane patents was still in operation. Martin and the other pioneers had no hope of succor without remedial legislation; which was not to come. Such was to be the experience of the inventor of the retractable chassis, the collapsible and retractable pontoons, aerodynamic control and airplane safety motors.

Twenty-two of Martin's inventions were to appear on all modern airplanes, born of his brain and appropriated from him, to fly the skies over his gray head while, on the verge of starvation, he fought for his American rights.

"But there is justice when the people are aroused," the General reassured Martin. "I'm going down a different road from yours. Our roads will converge again. Get your information from the inventors, flyers, shop workers. I'll fight it out from the inside. You'll see my rocket's red glare, Jim, no matter how dark it may get."

Mitchell got down doggedly to his task. As Assistant Chief of the Army Air Service he was compelled to depend upon the approval of his superiors for the slightest of the changes he had in mind. His first recommendation was a memorandum, blazing with indignation, demanding the elimination of the "flying coffins" from the Air Arm. In it he described crisply what was happening even then on the training fields; airmen being killed almost daily in the DH4's. His sulphurous message reached the General Staff, but was thrown in the wastebasket.

He followed it up with an emphatic demand to change the position of the gasoline tanks forward in the machines in order to increase the safety factor in case of a crash. Men were still being burned alive when they fell, with the tanks of gasoline on top of them. Again, he was ignored by his superiors.

Almost daily, Mitchell's "emergency recommendations" were shot into the War Department like bullets from a marksman:

Aviation mechanics should be given a status different from that of the ordinary soldier in order to protect the lives of the flying personnel. Air transports should be made available for the carrying of air units. Combined air maneuvers should be staged to test coast defenses. Methods of protection against air raids in inhabited localities, including alarm signals, refugee rationing and medical assistance, should be devised. Provision should be made for a meteorological department in the Air Service. Commercial aviation should be encouraged to provide plane pilots for use in the event of a national emergency. A force of expert airplane mechanics should be trained. Closer co-operation should be established between the Air Service and Chemical Warfare Division.

The use of amphibian planes should be recognized for rescue work. At the earliest possible time, modern all-metal bombing planes should be acquired. Development of air routes throughout North and South America should be immediately started. The manufacturing of airplane landing-equipment, such as skis for ice or snow-covered grounds, should begin at once, with the training of airmen under extreme cold weather conditions. Also, an intensive study of flying fog-hazards in Alaska: and above all, an immediate Air Program for an adequate air defense of the Pacific Coast.

After the first two weeks of these recommendations (every one of which was to have a direct bearing on the Second World War), the War Department, including Wilson's Secretary of War, Newton D. Baker and the General Staff concluded that the Air Chief's zeal had unbalanced him.

Groggy under the deluge of memos, Army chiefs decided that his suggestions were too ridiculous to consider. Mitchell, conferring with a member of the Staff during this period, asked him, "What is the Staff doing with my recommendations? I haven't heard about any one of them. I think they're important to the country."

His superior laughed. "We're filing 'em."

With the exception of the recommendation to encourage commercial aviation to produce pilots for a war emergency, all other suggestions from Mitchell were ignored as fanciful flights of imagination. Later, he was to testify to all this under oath. The General pulled his belt in another notch. He had had in his mind from the time of his arrival from France an idea as startling as it was to be dramatic.

He was convinced that airplane development would make all navies obsolete and he cast his eye upon the naval war prizes which had been turned over to the United States after the war.

"The people can be awakened," he told his immediate superior, Major General Mason M. Patrick, a man who couldn't fly but who was in sympathy with his assistant.

"If I can get the High Command to let me bomb a battleship," Mitchell said, "the whole country will understand what this all means. If I sent a battleship to the bottom with air bombs, which I am convinced I can do, perhaps we'll stop wasting billions of dollars for these museum pieces and spend the money on planes. Battleships are through!"

This recommendation had the effect of an earthquake upon the War and Navy departments. Josephus Daniels, Secretary of the Navy, gasped when he read it. Mitchell, years later, recalling the commotion with amusement, said an aide had quoted Daniels as having spluttered on that occasion: "Good God! This man should be writing dime novels!"

But Mitchell's request for battleship prizes to be used for air bombings had been submitted with silent approval and advice from a surprising quarter. Old naval men quaked when they learned of the influential nature of the Air Chief's support.

Rear Admiral William Sowden Sims, brilliant naval strategist, who had been in command of the American World War fleets in European waters, had returned home with the conviction that battleships were vulnerable from the air and that, in wars to come, would deteriorate into floating death traps, floundering and helpless under airplane bombardments.

He believed the only ship of the future of any use in sea engagements would be the fast airplane carrier. Mitchell had gained a tremendous ally whose firm views and knowledge of shortsighted men in power were to have much to do in helping him to demonstrate his idea.

As Mitchell told of this phase of his battles:

"Admiral Sims had a contempt for politics in the Navy. He accused the 'Daniels Cabinet,' as he described it, of deliberately obstructing the development of an efficient Air Service. Sims thought it was a piece of insanity for the country to be without a driving, intelligent Air policy. He told me I had done an inestimable service in bringing the controversy of aircraft and sea craft to the surface and that if I didn't become too impatient, I would get the battleships.

"In his quiet way he helped to bring the tests about and should be given full credit for what he did. He supported me in blasting from the sea all the theories to which he had devoted his life. In my estimation, he makes Mahan look like a powder-monkey. In my presence, more than once, he expressed his contempt and disgust with the Navy's attitude of always resisting the introduction of a new weapon. But he could never agree with me about a united Air Service."

The opposition to Mitchell's proposed air tests on capital ships was to spread far beyond the scope of the Navy Department before he could demonstrate to the world that dreadnaughts were outmoded and doomed.

One of the chief arguments he had to surmount came from high officials of the Wilson administration who feared that a successful demonstration might have a disastrous effect on the steel industry, whose leaders and lobbyists were clamoring for $70,000,000 battleship-contracts as an impetus to business and employment.

In order to permit the controversy to rock itself to sleep, the General turned to another idea, but not before he had made a final and particular request to the High Command for the use of two powerful prize ships for his demonstrations: the great dreadnaught Ostfriesland of the Jutland class and the heavy cruiser Frankfort.

The other idea which he decided to advocate publicly in the meantime was to arouse such violent protests from both Baker and Daniels as to make his battleship bombing project almost impossible while they remained in office.

Upon his own responsibility the Air Chief launched a campaign for a unified Air Service under the command of a Secretary for Air in the Cabinet.

Immediately he found himself in hot water with Secretary Baker. The activity stirred the War and Navy Departments to their profoundest depths and was the immediate cause of an explosive row between Daniels and the Secretary of War upon whom the Navy Chief called, with vigor, to muzzle Mitchell by disciplinary measures.

The General had driven his superiors almost to apoplexy by appearing completely without authorization before the Congressional Committee considering the new Army bill, to advocate his views. There is good indication that he impressed the Committee members, who actually had his project written into the Army Appropriation bill of 1920.

Army friends of Mitchell's, in touch with the War Department, urged him, in their anxiety, to take a vacation until the General Staff had recovered its equilibrium. As a matter of fact, he went off, with a wide grin, on a fishing trip in a seaplane especially equipped for the purpose.

"Mitchell's audacity had thrown Secretary Daniels into a violent rage which for days burst out as soon as he came into his office. According to excellent authority, he fell back upon his vocabulary as a former editor to describe Mitchell as "reptilian."

He believed Baker should have curbed the Air Chief long since and referred to the Secretary of War as "that Newtie Cootie."

The official correspondence between Baker and Daniels over the Mitchell affair, which may now be disclosed after twenty-two years, shows how deep-seated were the roots, even then, of the animosity toward the General's Air program.

It shows more: the determination of the War and Navy departments to prevent officers from telling the truth to the Congress of the condition of national defense. The letters are important, as in them were shown, full-grown, the blindness, obstinacy and stupidity which were to afflict the Army and Navy bureaucracy and to be reflected in its scoffing and tragic viewpoint of the Air Arm until Pearl Harbor.

Wrote Daniels to Baker, on May 27, 1920:

Dear Mr. Secretary:

The printed copy of the recent hearings before the Committee on Military Affairs of the Senate has come to my notice, and I have to invite your attention to certain incorrect, incomplete and misleading statements which reflect discredit upon naval aviation.

You will have in mind our declared intention that there shall be complete coordination and co-operation between the Air Services of the Army and the Navy.

Needless to say, you will understand the impossibility of ensuring harmonious co-operation or of retaining the sympathy of Congress, if individuals belonging to either the Army or Navy discredit in public hearings the sister service of the other Department of the Government.

You will recall that on December 17, 1919, I addressed a letter to you regarding the testimony given before the Committee on Military Affairs of the House of Representatives, the propriety of which seemed questionable, and I have now again to invite attention to the misleading character of the evidence which again has been submitted to legislators.

In the figures presented, indicating a great duplication in stations, experimental work and general overhead, there is glaring inaccuracy. They are not only misleading, but reflect directly and seriously upon the work of the Aeronautical Board, as well as upon the Air Services of the Army and Navy. The estimated savings appear to be purely speculative. That they should be presented to Congress at this time as facts are more than unfortunate.

The statements of General Mitchell can only be construed as reflecting most unfavorably upon the Navy, and coming from an officer in his position, as already mentioned, cannot fail to carry weight and to create wrong impressions. Effort to build up the service to which an officer is attached is entirely commendable, but when the effort discredits another branch of the government, it cannot be justified.

I have to repeat a recommendation made to you in my letter of December last—that Congress has the right to obtain accurate information in its hearings, and to point out that insofar as the Navy is concerned, accuracy would best be secured through direct testimony obtained from those in the Navy and not from evidence such as that which unfortunately appears to have been given to

the Senate Military Affairs Committee in this instance.

In closing, I may add, Mr. Secretary, that it would seem most unfortunate, that the efforts of the War and Navy Departments and of the great majority of officers of the Army and Navy to coordinate the work of our Departments and to continue the co-operation which has existed in the past should be interfered with by an individual or individuals. It would seem particularly unhappy at this time when there is so much constructive work confronting both the Army and Navy in aeronautical matters.

Secretary Baker kept that letter on his desk nearly a month before replying. Finally, on June 24, 1920, he answered Daniels as follows:

From: The Secretary of War.
To: The Secretary of the Navy.
Subject: Hearings before Congressional Committee relative to Aviation.

1 - I desire to acknowledge receipt of your letter of May 27, 1920, relative to certain hearings of Brigadier General William Mitchell before the Committee on Military Affairs of the Senate.

2 - In this connection you are advised that the Department has recently issued instructions which outline its policy with reference to

Congressional hearings. While it is the purpose of these instructions to authorize a reasonable and proper freedom of speech on the part of Army officers testifying before the authorized Congressional Committee, they do not contemplate nor permit the making of statements, especially with reference to the other coordinate executive departments, which may reasonably serve to discredit or to reflect upon the work of these departments.

3 - Such statements on the part of subordinate officers or of anyone in the executive departments cannot but militate against the attainment of the efficient co-operation between the Departments which is essential to the proper consideration and development of policies affecting more than one Department, and it is believed that steps which already have been taken by the War Department will ensure that the policy of the Department, as above outlined, will be conformed with hereafter by officers of the Army who have occasion to testify before the Senate Committees relative to aviation matters.

After he had read Baker's letter, Secretary Daniels ordered his staff to keep "Mitchell's ideas" out of the office. "And I don't want to hear any more about sinking battleships with air bombs," he roared.

Mitchell quoted him as having said: "That idea is so damned nonsensical and impossible that I'm willing to stand on the bridge of a battleship while that nitwit tries to hit it from the air!"

Soon after Baker had replied to Daniels, Mitchell was summoned to the War Department and taken severely to task by the Secretary of War, himself. Mitchell described Baker's words, much later, as a "first-class tongue-lashing."

The little Secretary was smarting at the time under the blistering attacks of the press concerning the billion-dollar aviation scandal. He wanted to forget about airplanes, and he said so plainly.

"This administration has less than another year to go," he said, "and I probably will not be here after that, but while I remain at this desk, General, I shall see to it that you are prevented from stirring discontent among the Army and Navy personnel. What you have done is more than disturbing to me—and it may have far-reaching effect."

The Secretary was not to live long enough to learn how far-reaching the effect would be. When he had curtly nodded Mitchell out, he had closed his door on one of the truly historic movements in the evolution of America. Had Mitchell's plan gone through there probably would have been a Department of Air, as there is of War, Navy, Commerce and other divisions of the government.

With an Air Secretary in the Cabinet and with airmen at the head of U.S. Air, the United States would have been prepared to meet the conditions of modern war twenty-one years later. Until the end of the Wilson Administration, Mitchell made no headway in his effort to win the High Command over to his cause. The President, who had been startled in 1917 to discover that the United States had but fifty-five airplanes, had long ago forgotten the possibilities of Air Warfare. He had a better program, a League of Nations, which was to put an end to all wars.

Then airplanes might be developed to carry merry passengers around a peaceful world. Mitchell attempted to see him but was advised that the Chief Executive was on the verge of a nervous breakdown. Newspapers were referring to him as "the sick man of Europe." [Riffing on a 19th Century phrase which referred to the perpetually plagued Balkan nations.]

Friends suggested that Mitchell might explain his position to a busy young man in the Navy Department, Franklin D. Roosevelt, Assistant Secretary of the Navy. This move, they said, might help to soften the wrath of Daniels. The young man, it was said, was a good diplomat.

But Roosevelt had other matters in mind. He was devoted to the League of Nations and had already offered himself to campaign for it. A place, some leaders said, might be found for him on the Democratic ticket. A Vice Presidential candidate with the name of Roosevelt, it was argued, would add undeniable strength to the efforts of the party.

The future President was to climb on the bandwagon with James M. Cox in a futile fight for the League. The campaign was not to be remembered as having been concerned with airplanes.

Twenty years were to pass before Roosevelt was to cry for 60,000 airplanes a year, bombers, fighters, interceptors, and which would not then be enough to defend Democracy in a sprawling war all over the world. Mitchell, by his directness of manner and his persistency, had won for himself many friends in Congress where he continued to appeal for funds for aircraft improvements. The idea of bombing a battleship could not be shaken from his mind.

With his airmen he had been conducting bombing experiments in the upper Chesapeake Bay, near Aberdeen, Maryland, where detonations killed thousands of fish, tore up the bottom of the seabed and stopped traffic in the surrounding regions for days at a time. He kept up his tests, ignoring all protests, until he was convinced that he could announce definitely to the Congress that he could sink any battleship in existence or any that could be built.

The element of time played in his favor. The German prizes of war, turned over to the United States, had to be destroyed after a certain limited period of study to conform with the requirements that they were not to be added to our naval strength.

The General went over the heads of the War and Navy Departments and appealed to the Congress for a special resolution authorizing the President to designate the chief war prizes as targets for air bombs!

Meanwhile, President Harding and his Ohio friends had moved to Washington to "take the country over," as some editors charitably described it. Being familiar with the machinations of the Ohio group in the aircraft conspiracy, Mitchell was downcast for the first time since his return from the wars.

His Air program, he felt, would have to depend on oily political considerations. But shrewd newspapermen advised him that the new administration was not opposed to headlines calculated to draw readers away from the criticism already being leveled at the Harding crowd. For this reason, they thought his idea had a chance.

Opposing Mitchell's sea tests, however, was the same board of scoffing admirals who held under their thumbs the new Secretary of the Navy, Edwin Denby, who assumed, like a chameleon does its colors, the attitude of the gentleman in the cocked hat toward the proposed bombings.

One afternoon he received word from the White House that favorable consideration of Mitchell's idea would not be displeasing to the President. He showed the note to his aides who burst into laughter. The admirals shuddered when they were informed of it. Denby, who was ignorant of the moves of Admiral Sims behind the scenes, looked upon the proposal as utterly fantastic. The double-dealing and contemptible chicanery resorted to by members of the High Command to block the air crusader's experiments, when it heard that Mitchell had impressed the Congress, would be almost impossible to describe. In deference to those who stooped low from high places and who are still alive waiting for the news of great toe-to-toe naval engagements in these distraught times, they will not be detailed here.

Some weeks after the new administration had settled down, a quiet and informal poker party, which was becoming part of the President's routine after the daily grind, assembled in the mysterious little mansion not far from the White House. The hideaway was to become notorious, the topic of secret gossip, the scene of a murder and finally the subject for novels.

Benedict M. Holden, a well-known Connecticut lawyer and astute politician, serves as authority for the conversation which took place over the cards on that occasion. He knew Harding well enough to handle the pasteboards with him and to call him "Warren," if not Gamaliel. It was to Holden that Harding had said with his feet on his desk, when the lawyer had visited him at the White House to congratulate him upon his election: "Ben, now I can tell any son-of-a-bitch in the United States to go to hell!"

During a lull in the poker game, presumably while the cards were being dealt, the President was answering a few questions in order to keep the folks posted on the state of the Union. According to Holden, the Chief Executive had much on his mind. There was the matter of Miss Nan Britton who was later to write a book naming him as the father of her child.

There was also Poincaré who wanted his support against England for his seizure of the Ruhr. Besides that, the boys were going a bit too far with honest graft. This business of running the country was much more serious than he had implied when he was asked by reporters how he had been nominated: "We drew a pair of deuces and filled."

There were many reasons for the President's look of surprise and relief when he raised his eyes from his cards to answer a popular query that changed the trend of the conversation.

"Warren, are you going to let Mitchell bomb the battleship?"

"It's no longer an executive problem," he replied. "The people have spoken. Congress has authorized the President to turn the war prizes over to the General for sea targets. The Admirals are having apoplexy. Maybe the excitement will change the complexion of the headlines. It won't do any harm to let the General fly over those boats. There's one thing about Mitchell, he's the most persistent cuss in the Service. I'm tired of this 'Air row' anyhow, and as Commander-in-Chief of the Army and Navy I hope his bombs settle the argument.

"Denby thinks the idea is crazy, but I notice he hasn't offered to stand on deck under the bombs, as Daniels did. Mitchell is going to have the Ostfriesland and the Frankfort to work on. It's going to be a great show. I wish I could go on the party. We're going to have a picnic boat off the Virginia Capes to watch it. If you boys care to offer any odds, I'll take a bet that he sinks the battleship."

4 - THE OSTFRIESLAND AND MR. KATSUDA

AT LANGLEY FIELD, CENTER OF THE Army establishment at Tide-water Virginia, General Billy Mitchell, the only visible inhabitant of the post was watching the sun coming up in a flash of crimson splendor. He had had but little sleep.

His orderly said the Air Chief had not taken off his uniform since the previous day. Two days before, on July 18, 1921, under his leadership, his airmen had sunk the tough German cruiser Frank-fort with straight hits in the open sea. Observers and commentators upon the test agreed unanimously that it had added very little to the knowledge of modern warfare. Most of them called it "Mitchell's fool-luck."

Admirals at the Navy Department cried, "It was only a cruiser ly-ing helplessly under him! He's been yelling about sinking battleships. He'll find that a different proposition. He'll sink himself, eventually!"

Far back at the Post, behind its airplanes and hangars, a bugle sounded familiar morning music. Men rose to it, running into the grooved routine of a new Army day. Lieutenant Farewell Bragg, an early riser, had hurried to the General's quarters, but it appeared that his bed had hardly been disturbed. Bragg, a youngster of whom Mitchell was fond, because of his quick intelligence, discovered his chief at the edge of the Field, talking to himself.

His hands behind his back, the General seemed to be address-ing the sun:

"This is the day, old boy. Good weather is the only condition we can expect in our favor. The machines, God knows, are not equipped for it. They're making us fly sixty miles out to make it tougher. Chase those clouds away. Give us a high ceiling. We'll do it yet. We're going to sink a battleship! It can be done!"

Bragg stood a few paces back, almost in awe. He might have sworn his Chief was praying to the sun. Suddenly the lieutenant found himself looking into a pair of eyes, slits of fire, burning in a face alive with alertness.

The boys slept soundly," Billy snapped. "That's a good sign. They're not downhearted, anyhow, about that Ostfriesland business. They'll need iron in their blood today. We're going to do this thing. Tell them to eat lightly; not too much coffee. Get mine ready; that's all I'll have," and after a moment of hesitation, as the lieutenant saluted and wheeled about, "tell them today we're going to sink the Ostfriesland, by God, or we're not coming back! I've worked out a new plan. We're going to send her to the bottom with 2,000-pound bombs and to hell with the brass heads who want us to drop cream puffs!"

A chorus of cheers from the mess hall, a few minutes later, drew a smile from Billy's tight lips.

"They've got the news," he murmured.

Still looking at the sun, he swung his arms about in gestures of calisthenics and, with the old stride of a soldier, marched back to his quarters, from which he soon emerged, refreshed and laughing. He loved to do the impossible. This was the time for it.

The events of the previous day had developed enough disappointments to harass Mitchell's mind. Complying with the Congressional order, the High Command of the Navy had permitted him to attempt the sinking of the Ostfriesland but had held him under strict orders to use nothing of heavier weight than small bombs of 230 pounds, as ineffectual as firecrackers on the mass of steel.

After a passionate plea, he wheedled from the Navy a few bombs weighing 550 and 600 pounds, but try as they might, his airplanes, including the DH's which he loathed, had failed to sink the battleship. To add to his discomfiture, he had received peremptory orders, a few minutes before his attempt, to operate at an altitude of 10,000 feet.

"God damn their brainless skulls," he had exploded, in pardonable wrath.

As a matter of fact, he had no bombers to make the height. He declared at the time, and repeated it in testimony before Commissions of Inquiry later, that the orders he had been given were a deliberate attempt to hamper his chances of success. But, he added with pride, one of his airmen, in heroic desperation had succeeded somehow in ascending 11,000 feet, taking his life in his hands in his frail machine and had hit the old battleship twice, although without doing much damage. Naval observers had called the feat, "a couple of lucky shots."

Billy, nevertheless, saw in the accomplishment a remarkable achievement under the conditions which controlled it. Big bombs, he was convinced would finish the job. This had spurred him, despite the obstacles shoved in his way at every turn, to prove with deadly accuracy that the heaviest type of dreadnaught could be sunk from the air.

"I had that feeling about it down to my toes," he said.

Mitchell had begged the government for many months to obtain planes operating with two or three engines each. He pleaded for appropriations in Congress for these machines, pointing out, sometimes during shouted arguments, that while America was ignoring this progress, European nations were already developing these types.

On July 20, 1921, the day the air crusader was to make his final attempt to sink the German battleship, the Army and Navy were without even one type unit of the latest foreign planes on which to base the future development of American aircraft.

Yet Billy Mitchell was visualizing huge aircraft carriers, loaded with 150 fighting planes, some carriers even transporting bombers to an objective 2,000 miles away. He was convinced the time was coming when lighter-than-air craft would be used as aerial carriers as well as those supporting air fighters on the seas. In other words, he believed dirigibles might be constructed to release fighting planes in midair.

"This problem," he would add, "has been the subject of study for a long time."

But the friends of his rank in the Army who liked him as a pleasant, affable companion, listening in boredom to his favorite topic, invariably launched at dinner parties where charming women preferred light repartee, would pat him on the back soothingly to get him off the subject.

Such talk always had the same ending: "You're all right, Billy. Don't get cracked about flying. You're too good a fellow. The war is over. Let's have another."

Mitchell was to make his second attempt on the Ostfriesland, witnesses crowded upon the decks on the old naval transport Henderson, sixty miles off the Virginia Capes, watching the General's flyers attempting the impossible with small bombs of deliberately restricted weight, had been so little impressed that a number of important observers decided to ignore further experiments and go home.

General John Pershing, standing close to John W. Weeks, Secretary of War, shook his head in derision as the small bombs failed miserably to dent the dreadnaught.

"I doubt if I shall waste more time on this croquet game tomorrow," he remarked to Weeks. "And what if he did hit the battleship? It couldn't sink her. And where would planes come from, assuming our fleet was in the turmoil of a fighting engagement in the middle of the ocean? Is anybody foolish enough to believe that boats could take squadrons of airplanes within the zone of a thundering battle between super-dreadnaughts, which couldn't even be dented? Mitchell did a good job for us in France, but at best it was just good scouting in the air on a grand scale."

Pershing's arguments so impressed Weeks that he decided to stay away also on the next day. The Secretary and the General had come to Old Point on a rocking destroyer, a trip of some discomfort, and placidly they settled themselves ashore, away from the blinding sun, cool drinks at their elbows, to await the news that this foolishness off the Capes was over. Some hours later, they heard the reverberations of terrific explosions, echoing across the sea for sixty miles.

Pershing, with a puzzled expression turned to the Secretary.

"What the blazes do you think that was?" he asked Weeks. "That didn't come from any 600-pound bombs."

"By God," Weeks replied heatedly, "if Mitchell violated orders by taking up anything heavier we'll put him on the carpet! He knows what he's supposed to use. Where would we be if he could sink the Navy?"

A few retired admirals in the comfortable shade put their glasses down to grunt in approval. One of them was sufficiently impressed with the conversation to repeat it.

But Pershing, who knew the din of battle through unerring ears, had been right. He had heard a sound greater than mighty winds, louder than the dash of oceans, a sound which in two decades was to signalize the disappearance of dreadnaughts as a weapon of naval war.

But it conveyed no meaning to him. Billy Mitchell and his Army airmen, whose unpredictable planes had left their shore base with bombs of 2,000 pounds, disregarding most of the orders of the armchair admirals and the "brass heads" of the War Department, as he called them, had climbed as high as it was safely possible with their loads.

The General had instructed his men to use their own judgment about altitude.

"Get into this thing," he said, "as if we had to sink an enemy ship attacking one of our ports. If we were at war, we would have to risk anti-aircraft. We wouldn't think of climbing 10,000 feet to dodge the job, even if we could get up there. None but cowards would leap behind a cloud. Do you understand me?"

Amid the roar of motors and the cheers of his men he pointed to the sea and climbed into his machine. They were off across a stretch of sixty miles of ocean in inferior planes which would have meant disaster for every man-jack of them if their engines had balked. The General was flying his control ship, the Osprey, a two-seater DH, and was accompanied by Captain "Wingbone" Street of the Army Air Corps.

Off the Virginia Capes, the transport Henderson rolled patiently in a sea which could not have been described as calm. The ship was still crowded, but many dignitaries, tired of peering into the sky under the hot sun, had gone below for heated discussion and whistle-wetting from refreshments whose potency had not been defiled by Prohibition. Bets were laid that Mitchell would never accomplish his purpose. In two instances, at least, some of the arguments led to blows.

One man who had expressed a searching interest in the experiment was a shrewd and very correct Englishman, Air Commodore Francis Charlton of the British Navy.

"The question," he said adjusting his monocle and putting down his Scotch and splash, "is not whether this imaginative fellow will accomplish his purpose. It is rather what will happen to this blooming world if the chap actually does it. Do you realize history may be made today, gentlemen?"

Suddenly the crowd of drinkers below were stirred by shouts from the deck.

Planes were roaring overhead.

All clambered up on deck and made for the rails from which the great Ostfriesland, swinging with her vast steel bosom exposed to the sky in German defiance, could be seen plainly by good eyes without glasses.

Admirals on board, although indulging their doubts, had made sure that the spectacle should be viewed from a zone of safety. Perhaps the battleship by some fluke, might be struck. None of them expected the massive vessel to be sunk.

Least of all were the observers on the Henderson aware that the roaring planes directly above them were armed with 2,000-pound bombs. For their peace of mind, it was probably just as well. They might all have ducked below and denied everything that happened.

The operation was not to keep the observers long in suspense. From a height of possibly 6,000 feet, a missile suddenly dropped like a plummet from one of Mitchell's whining machines. The packed Henderson's passengers heard a deafening explosion which echoed over the sea and they saw a terrifying wall of water which almost shut off the Ostfriesland from their vision.

Planes now were following each other over the target, maneuvering for the kill, circling about, coming back and releasing bombs from primitive racks.

After an impenetrable cloud of smoke had lifted, the dreadnaught could be seen to have received her death wound. More bombs from the circling planes with straight, shattering hits, made the battleship rock and shudder.

A Japanese guest, in diplomatic attire, on board the Henderson , the Hon. G. Katsuda, member of the House of Peers of Tokyo, chattered to a companion of his own race, wetting his lips and hissing with excitement. Holding a stopwatch as he gripped the rail, he nodded off the seconds. He did not have to count long after the bombs began to strike.

In precisely twenty minutes, the Ostfriesland had been sent to the bottom. Some observers on the Henderson were so overwrought at the sight that they wept. While other machines circled about, one plane hovered over the sea giant to give it a figurative coup-de-grace as her beak disappeared under the sea. The group of flyers drew closer together, circled the lone plane, dipped to it in graceful salute and raced for shore.

The solitary machine climbed almost straight into the air with a blasting snort of triumph, performed a wide arc and dove upon the Henderson until those aboard ducked involuntarily with fright. But the plane leveled off, passed over the ship, turned and spun slowly around it in a narrow circle.

Billy Mitchell at the controls, leaned perilously far out of its cockpit, and waved his hand to the gasping crowd. It was like him. You could see a devilish grin under his goggles. Suddenly with a choppy military salute, he swerved about and tore off after his boys.

General Pershing and Secretary Weeks were too far away to hear the spontaneous cheers and throat-bursting outcries of acclaim which continued from the Henderson until Billy Mitchell, streaking for Virginia, was a speck in the sky.

One grimy boiler-room enthusiast blew the transport's whistle until he had to be dragged from it. Diplomats, high army officers, over-correct Admirals, Senators and Congressmen, European military attaches, shouted their congratulations and waved handkerchiefs at the vanishing flyer. There was on board the Henderson at least one man of sufficient imagination to visualize what this dramatic accomplishment might do to mankind's tools of destruction. He was the polite and communicative Mr. G. Katsuda who had been doing an excellent job of making a good impression on American editors and chambers of commerce.

He did not hesitate to point out that Japan was one of the great customers of the United States and that his country would indubitably be in the market if America proposed to build airplanes capable of sinking battleships as a result of Mitchell's demonstration. The experiment seemed to impress him as an imaginative piece of advertising on a grand scale.

One alert reporter of the occasion, Daniel D. Bidwell of the Hartford Courant, erstwhile passenger on Henry Ford's peace ship, globe trotter of note and an ardent believer in Homer Lea's prophecies of a Japanese invasion of the United States, saw in the excitement of Mr. Katsuda the source of interesting stories for his newspaper and some good information for the future.

Mr. Katsuda, besides his membership of the Emperor's House of Peers had much to say, it seemed, in the Imperial Japanese Parliament. He was also chairman of the City Assembly of Kobe and was touring America with a less voluble fellow traveler, the Hon. G. Shibuta who represented the Kobe Chamber of Commerce. The Japanese visitors introduced themselves with gold-engraved cards. They seemed to know something about photography and had kept four powerful cameras clicking during the Ostfriesland's death throes.

"Very great experiment, profoundly exciting," said Mr. Katsuda to Mr. Bidwell. "I must put in cable for very great Japanese newspapers as eyewitness. Very fortunate to be here. Our people will cheer your great Mitchell and, you may be sure, will study his experiments. We respect American inventions. There is much to learn here."

Mr. Shibuta agreed with bows as he wrapped his precious camera in a large silk handkerchief. Mr. Katsuda was to lose no time in writing an article which soon appeared in the Sunday magazine section of a highly regarded New York newspaper, with the following sentiments beneath a large heading and, of course, carrying Mr. Katsuda's name and all his titles:

"A great deal of good paper has been wasted in the past ten years upon talk of possible war between America and Japan. We are satiated with this sort of talk. To us Japanese it seems strange that any intelligent person could imagine that Japan with her scanty resources, her inadequate industrial equipment and with her wholesome respect for the American Nation, would be stupid enough to commit national suicide by waging a hopeless as well as a meaningless war against America."

But Mr. Katsuda had not included in his goodwill essay what he had told the reporter Bidwell in an off-the-record chat about the subject of war between America and Japan:

"Should there be such a war America would have to fight it a long way from home. It would be quite a distance to fly to sink battleships, as without a doubt it appears now they can be sunk, from the air. It would be gravely embarrassing to the American people if the ideas of your General Mitchell were more appreciated in Japan than in the United States. Gratitude is not one of the attributes of Democracy.

"As a representative of the Emperor, I may say that Japan will not forget your General's scientific contribution to the art of warfare. Perhaps it will strengthen our friendship for each other when we consider that your westernmost Aleutians are much less than 800 miles from Japan and that your honorable General predicts that soon that distance will be flown in three hours!"

5 - OLD ADMIRAL TUBAGUTS

A NIGHT OF JUBILEE, A DELIRIOUS LIONIZATION, followed Billy Mitchell's arrival from the Capes. His plane had hardly touched the ground at Langley Field when his air brigade lifted him into the air with rebel yells as, in high humor, he struggled to remove his goggles. For a time, discipline and superior rank were forgotten. With tears of joy, Lieutenant Farewell Bragg struggled through the crowd to protect his chief and help him to his quarters. Almost automatically a triumphal march of cheering men had been formed, striding with their General, embracing him, holding his arms, while up ahead someone banged on a bass drum the clock-like beats of a rousing Civil War recruiting song, guided shrilly by a proud veteran trumpeter:

> *"Get out the way*
> *For Old Dan Tucker!*
> *He's too late*
> *To get his supper!"*

The whole establishment took it up, bawling it out brazenly while Billy Mitchell, his feet hardly touching the ground, protesting, laughing, was carried along and deposited on his doorstep.

Hesitating, his face flaming with pleasure, he lifted his hand pleading for a moment of silence and with pardonable exultation, almost with the boyish satisfaction of having licked a bully, he shouted from his heart a remark, aimed rather at a system than at any personality, but which was bound to be repeated and add to the resentment growing against him in Washington: "Well, lads! I guess we showed Old Admiral Tubaguts something today!"

The sky rang with cheers and laughter. Mitchell's serenading aviators were too familiar with all the obstacles he had faced, the disgraceful attempts to frustrate his experiments, the chicanery he had had to bypass to get a battleship for a target. The Air Chief once again quieted his air-bombardiers who clung to his words as those of a prophet, "I don't want to steal Napoleon's stuff," he said seriously, "but in the war to come, and you will see it, God will be on the side of the heaviest air force. [Voltaire: "God is on the side of the big battalions."] What we did to the Frankfort and the Ostfriesland is what will happen from the air to all warships in future wars! And don't you forget it. Keep your eye on the sky!"

Somehow, Mitchell managed to slip inside his door with the help of Bragg while the crowd stormed outside, hailing their hero. To these men, as to the General himself, for that matter, all battleships had suddenly become subordinate to the airplane and all navies obsolete. Many of these enthusiasts under the crusader's training were to become daring air leaders of the next war when America was to shout for the planes without which victory would not be possible. In his office, panting and wiping his face, the General prepared the paperwork of his next ocean experiments, Bragg passing him the documents which had been reluctantly signed by his superiors to permit the continuance of his demonstrations.

Telegrams of congratulation were coming in. "We doff our caps to you. You have made good your predictions," groups of naval officers wired. A message from Major General Charles T. Menoher said: "You have made history." Of more significance was the message of Air Commodore Charlton of the British Navy who had seen the destruction of the dreadnaught with tense face, his eyes glued to his glasses, his monocle lost in his excitement: "This shot will ring around the world. I am leaving for England convinced you have shaken naval tactics to their foundation. May Lord Nelson rise from his tomb to smite me, if I am wrong."

Outside of Mitchell's office, the celebration continued. Night had fallen, and through his windows came the cheers, the pounding of drums, the reflection of red fire, and occasional rockets. The old Civil War song rang almost at a battle cry. The entire establishment was out in a wild parade. Mitchell peered out of his window. The field was a crimson glow silhouetting dark figures of prancing men.

Bragg, at the General's elbow, controlled his own emotions with difficulty. He had seen the bitter, sarcastic correspondence from his chief's superiors which had to be answered before this triumph could be accomplished; the endless haggling arguments, the doubts, the footless questions. The General sighed, yanked out a large handkerchief. His eyes were wet.

"Damn those boys," he said hoarsely, "tell them to go to bed before I spank 'em and put 'em into short pants. But, by God," and his voice trembled, "they did it with the DH's! And the other bombers weren't much better. Perhaps we can get something safer for them now."

The nation's newspapers, the next day, gave great prominence to the news of the sinking of the Ostfriesland. The New York Times treated the exploit as of first importance on its front page. As a matter of fact, the account had gone around the world, to be read by startled naval experts from London to Tokyo. Berlin's Gasschutz und Luftschutz, a publication of wide scientific authority, cabled Mitchell for a special article of 3,000 words.

Telegrams from book publishers begged for manuscripts. Magazine editors telephoned from New York to outbid each other for material. Billy Mitchell had become the man of the hour, dashing off his articles in longhand after his day's work was done. His energy seemed incredible. "I'm going to hit the hay for a little rest," he would say, after weary hours at his desk.

The editorial comments of the press amused him almost as much as the expressed opinions of some of the government authorities who had witnessed the bombing. Editorial writers were not ready to admit that the dramatic experiment proved anything. They approached the business as a timid bather trying the temperature of a cold pool with his toes. Headline writers, however, were enjoying a carnival. Mitchell was the newsiest single figure since the war.

Sinking the pride of the German Navy from the air made exhilarating copy even in Chinese, in which language, incidentally, it was printed in Shanghai and Canton with predictions that the achievement would throw the proposed Four-Power Naval pact into chaos.

The comments of some of the official witnesses on the Henderson showed an extraordinary lack of comprehension. Theodore Roosevelt Jr., Assistant Secretary of the Navy, who had predicted that the bombing attempt would be a comic failure, joined the chorus which shouted that Mitchell was "just lucky."

Said young Roosevelt: "I saw it all. In the first place Mitchell flew below the required 10,000 feet and violated his orders. Such an experiment without actual conditions of war to support it is a foolish waste of time. I once saw a man kill a lion with a 30-30 caliber rifle; under certain conditions, mind you. That did not impress lion hunters. That did not mean that a 30-30 rifle is a lion gun!"

The younger Teddy insisted that airplanes should not be considered capable of superseding more recognized means of attack and defense. They certainly were not to be considered superior to the "fortresses of the sea."

The attacks off the Capes, he reiterated, proved nothing because they had all been carried out under ideal conditions. Weeks, the Secretary of War, angrily refused before reporters to commit himself for airplanes as against battleships. As he told his New England friend, editor Clark of the Hartford Courant a few weeks later: "I'm not going to be stampeded by a circus performer. Mitchell is putting a lot of foolish ideas in the heads of the people, and one of these days we may have to get rid of him. I stand by Pershing's opinions, which are good enough for me. He won the war without even looking into an airplane, let alone going up in one. If they had been of such importance, he'd have tried at least one ride. He says you'll never be able to catch him flying around in those contraptions. We'll stick to the army on the ground and the battleships on the sea."

Edwin Denby, Secretary of the Navy, who had seen the Ostfriesland go down, with his eyes straining their sockets, indicated that he was beginning to doubt the complete supremacy of the battleship in years to come. As a one-time gunner's mate on the U.S.S. Yosemite during the Spanish-American war (his only naval experience), he was not ready to remove the bust of [Battle of Manila hero] Admiral [George] Dewey [1837-1917] from his desk. Sheepishly, he asked the boys of the press to forget the remarks he had made before the bombings began.

"Hell's bells," he said. "We all make mistakes. Mitchell has my congratulations. You can quote me as saying that scientific conclusions of value undoubtedly will result from these experiments. That's as far as I want to go."

It was as far as anybody in high responsibility in Washington wanted to go, even after Billy Mitchell had participated in and directed other exploits of the same nature with equal success, as he had predicted. But America, governed by an administration both stupid and corrupt, shrugged its shoulders.

The battleship admirals (William Sowden Sims excepted) and the steel lobby were powerful enough to muzzle honest government experts who desired to warn the country that Mitchell's demonstrations carried world-shaking significance. The fact remained, in the case of the Ostfriesland, that the side deck protective armor which, for years, it had been argued, would protect the vitals of a dreadnaught against any conceivable bomb, had been shattered by concussion caused by a missile dropped from the sky. The Ostfriesland's class had formed the German first battle-squadron in the historic sea fight of Jutland. Would all naval calculations have to be scrapped because of a persistent fanatic?

Experts at the New York Navy Yard, who had inspected the dreadnaught, one of Germany's surrendered vessels allocated to the United States after 1918, were aghast. The Navy already was revising its own construction blueprints after a study of all the details of the dreadnaught's construction and fittings. Turret and deck armor and side plates had been subjected to ballistic tests. Long reports had to be prepared and were not even half completed when Billy Mitchell had come along and sunk the battleship, including a lot of theories and statistics, in twenty (or four!) thundering minutes.

One man, who, four years later, was to clash with the flying crusader in violent conflict and become one of his bitterest enemies, saw in the bombings of 1921 perhaps more significance than any other official in the Navy Department. He was ['The Architect of Naval Aviation'] William Adger Moffett [1869-1933], an old Dewey man during the capture of Manila. Now director of the Bureau of Naval Aeronautics, with the rank of Captain, a fellow member of Billy Mitchell's in Washington clubs, he perceived that the flyer's audacious experiments presaged a great revolution in naval tactics. He urged that a program be launched immediately to build at least half a dozen airplane carriers, a provision which the Congress, in its new naval bill, swept into the wastebasket.

Not even one carrier was provided for in the measure. Moffett then recommended emphatically that aviators, with as many planes as could be managed, with some sort of catapult arrangement, should be put on all battleships, pending the time when carriers could be produced. A board of Admirals swept that suggestion from the table as a piece of foolishness, suspecting that Mitchell had prompted it. Moffett fought for his program until Mitchell, on his own authority, proclaimed that the entire aviation branch should be unified to include the Bureau of Aeronautics. The tragic feud which this announcement provoked between the two air enthusiasts was to continue until Moffett had paid for his own obstinacy with his life. He lived in fear of being reduced to obscurity should Mitchell's plans for a coordinated national defense become an accomplished fact.

The alarm was to spread to other small-minded men in authority. As active Director of Military Aviation, with an interested public daily at his elbow, Mitchell now took full advantage of his position as a recognized flying authority. Intolerant of the stupid and unimaginative, he flayed those in power who refused to recognize the airplane as a dominating arm of warfare. His crop of influential enemies, fighting for old traditions, old systems, ignorant of the potentialities of the aircraft which had been placed in their care for use and development, seemed powerless to combat him.

The people were on Mitchell's side in the great controversy which was to stretch through two decades. As early as 1910 Mitchell had said that America would be helpless in an air war and that an air fleet could wipe out all of New York City. Eleven years later he flew over the metropolis leading his bombers in a sham battle.

He announced blandly, as he landed from the flight, that his planes had suffered no casualties and that the whole city had been destroyed. This was, of course, a characteristic piece of humorous exaggeration, but there was enough truth in it to set many people thinking. He predicted a day when airplanes would fly at an un-heard-of speed of 250 miles an hour. Government experts broadly intimated that he was becoming unbalanced, but in less than ten years from the date of his prophecy, airplanes were to fly at the speed of 500 miles an hour.

To focus attention upon the dangers of aerial attack on America from across the Pacific, Mitchell created an apparently fanciful picture of a day when airplanes would fly regularly from China to San Francisco. Twenty years later, in 1935, a year before his death, he was to see this prediction come true when the first regular trans-Pacific airline was opened with the Philippine Clipper and the China Clipper planes. "They thought I was crazy," he said.

After the bombings off the Capes, Mitchell infuriated the Naval High Command by charging publicly that the official Navy report on the experiment had been changed to the detriment of the facts which his flyers had demonstrated. Time was to prove this accusation to be true before private Congressional hearings; but defense experts of the day, who could not, or would not, anticipate the airplane improvements which were bound to follow this devastating invention, continued to cling to the battleship as the most powerful instrument of war on the seas. High naval officials were now the crusader's avowed enemies, personally and professionally, actually conspiring to put a stop to his activities, even to stripping his uniform from him. They feared that his attacks might eventually undermine their own positions.

Meanwhile, steel magnates renewed their lobbying activities for more dreadnaughts. In this warfare against Mitchell, the heads of the aircraft monopoly naturally were aligned. At times he would thrust at them, armed as he was, with the facts of the billion-dollar airplane conspiracy which official Washington was making every effort to bury and forget in the dark pigeonholes of the War and Navy Departments. He met the growing opposition with an increasingly savage defense of his belief and faith in the airplane. The strength of Mitchell's conviction that battleships could be put out of action by airplane attacks is significantly illustrated in an article which he prepared for the National Geographic Magazine for March 1921, four months before he destroyed the Ostfriesland.

Preaching what was then looked upon as heresy in the military world, he wrote, "A direct hit by an aerial bomb on a battleship will break every electric light globe on the ship and throw her into absolute darkness below-decks; will disrupt telephone, radio, and interior communication systems; fill with noxious gases the fire-rooms, engine rooms, and all compartments ventilated by force draft; cause shellshock to the personnel practically all over the ship; will disrupt ammunition hoists, dislodge and jam turrets, dish upper decks, kill all personnel on upper decks, anti-aircraft gun crews, fire-control parties in the tops, or anyone standing on deck; will cause fire to break out, exploding all the anti-aircraft ammunition on upper decks.

"Heretofore projectiles from large cannon have been designed to pierce the armor of battleships, and then cause their effect by driving the fragments through the bulkheads and into various parts of the ship. Twenty-five such shots went clean through the German flagship Derflinger in the Battle of Jutland, but aside from killing 200 of the personnel, never destroyed the speed of this ship. These twenty-five shots altogether had no more than about 1,000 pounds of explosive in them. But one of our present air bombs, which weighs one ton and contains from 1,000 to 1,400 pounds of explosive, dropped on her from an airplane, would have wrecked this ship to such an extent as to put her completely out of action and end her usefulness as a war vessel."

Mitchell's achievement at sea resulted in a groundswell of enthusiasm among subordinate heads of departments of the Army and Navy. Encouraged by the crusader's zeal and his fight against politics in all branches of the armed services they sought him out at the risk of their own security to reveal conditions ranging from complete laxity to downright negligence in the Nation's defenses.

Soon the High Command of the Army and Navy was stunned by the General's demand, printed in newspapers from coast to coast, for a convulsive shake-up of the whole national defense system which he insisted must be reorganized and coordinated under a single responsible head as Secretary of Defense with three sub-secretaries for Air, Army and Navy. This idea, born of intelligence, foresight and courage, which many dispassionate observers believe America may have to adopt before the present war is won, agitated Mitchell's superiors into open antagonism against him.

From that time on, he was to be curbed and lashed and finally broken for his views. No one, perhaps until Pearl Harbor, and even after that, in high authority in the government was ready to admit that the Air Chief had riddled the concepts of sea war and land war and that giant bombing airplanes would constitute the heavy artillery of the future in far-reaching offensive strategy.

6 - ALASKA

FOR A FEW WEEKS, EARLY IN 1923, Billy Mitchell seemingly was too much occupied with the routine of his job to talk to the press. The air controversy slipped quietly from the front pages to repose in type which adorns blocks of advertising specified by ad space-buyers to appear "next to reading matter."

Gentlemen in the War Department enjoyed a breathing spell.

The General was spending more time at his quarters in Washington, keeping closely to his "paperwork." Late at night, old Army companions, permitted to drop into his rooms for a nightcap found him slowly revolving a large globe, tracing lines from the top of the world, jotting down distances. He would swing with quick strides to an immense map of Mercator's projection, then back again to the globe, his pencil returning to one point: Alaska.

"I see you're dying with curiosity," Mitchell said, raising his head above the group of visitors peering in bewilderment at his markings.

"I've got an idea for another book, but I'll let the War Department have some of it ahead of time. I don't want people to think I'm asleep. This country, by an act of Providence has been given every means of natural protection. All that is required for its security is imagination. The airplane is the greatest instrument ever invented to keep the mind busy. Tonight, with this globe in front of me, I've flown from Alaska to New York with a load of bombs and poisonous gas. I dropped my load and returned to Alaska without a stop!"

"Better have your nightcap, General, after that trip," Major "Happy" Arnold remarked wryly, while the rest joined in a good-natured laugh.

"All right, fellows," Mitchell nodded, pushing his work aside, "I'm going to put it down in writing for our brass heads to read, that Alaska is the most strategic springboard of offensive aerial warfare on earth. I'm going to ask them why they're not doing something about it."

He jumped from his chair and waved his finger around the top of the globe.

"From here," he said, touching Alaska, "we could reach out by air in all directions. Somebody else could, too, if we lost that territory. From Alaska, we could swoop down on Japan, following the long finger of the Aleutians. We're going to have, one of these days, aircraft powerful enough to defy the temperatures of the North Pole.

We'll be able to fly from Alaska in a straight line across the Arctic Sea to Norway. We'll be able to jump directly to Petrograd, or across Greenland to the British Isles, in a series of hops if necessary.

"Look at these stepping stones across the Atlantic. Going by way of Labrador, Greenland, Iceland and Scandinavia, or these islands north of Great Britain, the greatest sea hop is less than 500 miles. Now, turn to the other direction. Here, for instance, is a perfect bridge to Asia from our own possessions. Fifty-two miles of water separating Alaska from Siberia. It is along these routes that future invasions will come. Great bombing flights will sound the death-knell of naval bases as monuments of world empire. It will be air ba-ses from now on. The nation that possesses the best air fleets will possess a world empire.

"But," he added, "right now, I'm thinking of Alaska. In an air war, if we were unprepared, Japan could take it away from us, first by dominating the sky and creeping up the Aleutians. It could work both ways, of course. We could jump off from Alaska and reduce To-kyo to powder. But if we were asleep, without planes, Japan might well seize enough of Alaska to creep down the western coast of Can-ada. Then, we would be in for it.

"Homer Lea should have considered Alaska before drawing his conclusions that the Japanese could invade our Western coast through California. But he was so far ahead of our doddering strate-gists regarding a war with Japan that I can't quarrel with him. At least, his mind is traveling in the right direction. Of course, they're calling him a little hunchbacked fool, now."

This dynamic man's thoughts seemed always to lead on to pur-poses which went forth into actions.

"Things come to me," he would say, "and I'm prodded by a thou-sand devils until I have to act to stop wheels from rolling backward. Something urges me to push on, to keep the people from falling back. It's like flying over a battle line and feeling that you're pulling it along. How slowly people move on the ground. How slowly an army moves!"

In the early Spring of 1923, Mitchell wrote a list of private rec-ommendations about Alaska. He sent his paper, which was in the nature of a prophetic essay, to the War Department. Anticipating correctly that his views would be pigeonholed as usual by the Gen-eral Staff, he sent a copy of his conclusions to President Harding, who soon began to express an interest in the territory. Harding's in-quiries eventually reached into the War College, the General Staff and the whole gallery of "battleship admirals."

The High Command, which was beginning to hope that Mitchell's explosions had come to an end was again thrown into the familiar agitation. The General's statement was looked upon as calculated to launch a new controversy about airplanes.

His superiors in the War Department accused him of having encroached on the field of broad military strategy which, they asserted, was completely outside of his province. Moffett, director of the Bureau of Aeronautics, who had become a Rear Admiral, scoffed at Mitchell's predictions that flights could be made across the top of the world. Jealous of his authority, he insisted upon picking out an implication in the recommendations that he was not active or imaginative enough for his job.

"There could be no better indication than this flight of fancy," he remarked, "that Mitchell's mind is beginning to crack."

Yet, within two years of this episode, Amundsen reached the North Pole with two flying boats, returning in one with both crews. A year after this accomplishment, Commodore Richard Byrd and Floyd Bennett, in 1926, flew around the Pole in a three-engined monoplane. Captain G. H. Wilkins was to reach it in a Lockheed Vega. The Italians were less successful with Colonel Nobile's attempt with the airships Norge and Italia.

While Mitchell remained publicly silent about his Alaskan views, with which he did not intend at the time to regale the press for reasons of international diplomacy, he received word that President Harding desired to discuss the matter with him under circumstances of the strictest privacy.

As the General recalled the conference later, the Chief Executive had evidently been studying many reports about Alaska, which he seemed to look upon as some far-off land newly discovered.

"That was a great piece of business," Harding said, "when we bought that neck of the woods from the Russians for seven million bucks. I've been looking into it. We've got about $70,000,000 invested in the fishing trade up there. The salmon pack alone produces about $40,000,000 a year. Furs and skins brings over $4,000,000 a year. Think of the gold we took out of the place, more than three hundred million dollars' worth; and there's copper and silver, coal and oil. General, you're goddamned right about this business. What a grab that would be for Japan! And right now, we couldn't defend it. We've been asleep. I'm not going to forget this."

In June of 1923 Harding packed off for Alaska with a boatload of government officials and reporters. The expedition was to have a violent effect on Mitchell's future.

The General had not forgotten that he had been able, in spite of the opposition of his superiors, to demonstrate the power of the airplane over battleships during Harding's administration.

He was beginning to feel that Harding might support further aviation experiments and in his own peculiar way use his influence to revitalize the Air Force and quiet the opposition to Mitchell's program. The real motives behind Harding's Alaskan trip, on the other hand, may never be known. The President already was aware that the administration was saturated with corruption.

Albert Bacon Fall, his Secretary of the Interior, had been compelled to resign three months previously, after having secretly leased a choice naval oil-reserve to the scheming petroleum producer, Edward L. Doheny, who offered to show his appreciation of this one-sided bargain by building oil tanks for the Navy free of charge at Pearl Harbor.

Harding's regime, bankrupt of statesmanship, was shot through with graft. Scandals seemed to be breaking out everywhere. Perhaps it was as good a time as any for Harding to get away, to give the press something more savory to print.

But thoughts of airplanes and strategic defenses were soon swept from his mind when he reached the territory. He was staggered by news he received in a long letter written in code from Washington, which was to make him forget Alaska and the whole United States.

His handsome face had taken on the appearance of a death-mask when he called the reporters to his quarters and asked: "What can a President do when his best friends betray him?" He got as far as San Francisco, to die before he could be impeached.

Mitchell saw even less hope for his air policies under the new incumbent than he had under Harding. The airplane was bound to be nothing but an appendage of the Army and Navy while Coolidge sat in the White House.

The silent Vermonter had already expressed himself about "flying machines." He believed they might be useful for "scouting purposes." They had proved nothing in the last war, he said.

Tales soon reached Mitchell's ears that Harding's successor was displeased with the attention the press had been giving to "that air squabble," as he described it. The President saw nothing in it but a disruption of discipline, and had little trouble in finding in the High Command a quorum to agree with him. There were plenty of knife grinders in Washington to sharpen the steel that was to be plunged into Mitchell's back.

Meanwhile, you would find the General in the thick of arguments before Congressional Committees, pleading for appropriations for more and better planes.

His facts about the "flaming coffins," the billion dollars spent for 196 planes, the murderous crates in which airmen were compelled to train, the incompetence, the laxity eating like a cutworm into national defense, all went into the record of his testimony. Once-close Army friends now talked of his "over-zealousness" and began to shy away from him in order not to endanger their own positions.

Mitchell began to realize that his crusade was shrinking into a one-man job. But still he continued to flame into the news-consciousness of the people. His first book, Our Air Force, the Keystone of National Defense, which John Macrae of E. P. Dutton & Co., had encouraged him to write during this period, was reaching a thinking audience. Mail from his supporters all over the country was increasing.

Hoping for changes in the administration which might prove favorable to his cause, the General watched the backfire of the Teapot Dome scandal upon Coolidge's regime with intense interest.

Perhaps the upheaval might produce some single far-seeing figure in the Cabinet to whom he could appeal. Herbert Hoover, Secretary of Commerce under Harding and Coolidge apparently was not even remotely interested in the aviation campaign. His views on the limitation of armaments at that time would have relegated the airplane to the scrap pile. His face would light up occasionally over problems of flood relief.

Denby, Secretary of the Navy, whose interest in Mitchell's demonstrations appeared to be growing, bowed himself out of the National scene as a result of the Fall affair, insisting to the last that the Naval oil leases involved were legal. Coolidge, accepting his resignation, assured Denby that his honesty had not been impugned. Theodore Roosevelt, Jr., as Assistant Secretary clung to his job a few months longer, but in October of 1924 followed Denby out.

Mitchell groaned when he heard of the appointment of Denby's successor, a worthy gentleman named Curtis Dwight Wilbur, a California judge whose chief interest was juvenile-court work and who had waved goodbye to the Navy as soon as he had been graduated from the United States Naval Academy in 1888.

"How Coolidge happened to pick that bird," Mitchell remarked later, "is one of the fascinating mysteries of his Administration. He must have known less about airplanes than the peanut vendor in front of the White House. It reminded me of the story told about a bewildered civilian who was appointed Naval Secretary before the Civil War. He had never been on a boat and decided to look one over as soon as he assumed office. Walking on the deck of a naval vessel he peered into a hatchway with amazement and cried: 'By God, it's hollow!' "

MITCHELL NOW BECAME PRESSING ABOUT his Alaskan recommendations. The War Department received more of his views: suggestions for aviation developments in the territory with which he was personally familiar as a result of having laid miles of telegraph lines down the Yukon before the Wright brothers had made the world's first controlled flight in a power-driven machine.

It was all coming back to him. The airplane would save Alaska. Perhaps the idea had penetrated Harding's mind, but it was too late to speculate about that. The General Staff read Mitchell's fulminations without enthusiasm. His written appeals were to land in the barrels of the Emory building. Clerks flung them on piles of papers marked "too speculative to file," "too controversial for the records."

Finally, his superiors ignored the matter entirely.

"He's at it again," they said.

But Mitchell continued his bombardment: "With Alaska as a base of operations, America could dominate the entire world through air power. With ships flying across the Arctic we could reach any part of the world from which danger might emanate. It is the only base from which we could attack Japan."

The Air Chief called for a government department of Research and Experimentation, "so that the air service of the United States can be kept at the highest point of efficiency."

The appeal was thrown into the wastebasket as soon as it had been read. He referred to the aircraft industry as a "financial racket into which a generous government has poured millions of dollars."

His criticisms became open and vitriolic. At the Army and Navy Club, the Chevy Chase, his friends implored him to "pipe down." The comments of the "brass heads" were being repeated. "They're going to get you, Billy. They'll break you!" nervous companions warned him. Mitchell retorted by sounding an ominous prediction about commercial aviation: "There isn't a safe passenger plane in use in America today. Each should carry a cabin parachute, a resonance altimeter, a landing stick and automatic pilot equipment. People will listen to this after hundreds of the trustful have been sacrificed." It was to be as he had said.

The crusader occupied his time, aside from his Army duties by producing the first complete airways map in the United States (on which he had begun to work in 1920), recommending the locations for landing fields, keeping in his mind, always, the strategic points of air defense. It was to become the basic blueprint of sky transportation across the face of America.

Forgetting for a time the National controversy he had provoked, the Air Chief married, in October of 1923, Elizabeth Trumbull Miller, a young woman of high intelligence who had become devoted to his cause and whose rare understanding was to be his strongest anchor through the turbulent thirteen remaining years of his life.

It was the General's second marriage. Mrs. Mitchell flew with him over the Philippines, over Luzon, the Mariveles Mountain, Cavite Province and Bataan, places then unknown to the average American.

Mrs. Mitchell was with him when he discovered the sorry condition into which the Air Service had been permitted to fall in the Philippines and at Hawaii.

She helped him to prepare his reports which even then were to sound the warning of what was to prove to be tragically true nineteen years later when our heroic forces trapped with the Filipinos, called pathetically for the airplanes which after Mitchell's first insistence on their importance had not been furnished in sufficient numbers for the defense of our Far East possessions.

Eleven years later, Mitchell's Philippine and Hawaiian findings were fished out accidentally by War Department officials during a house cleaning expedition, from a barrel of papers in the cellar of the Emory Building, a warehouse for "unapproved records."

They were read with curiosity by the military finders, one of whom possessed sufficient consideration to return them to the air crusader with a line of tragic humor: "You can laugh at this stuff, now!"

This was seven years before a stunned people were to be asked by shaken government publicists to remember Pearl Harbor—seven years before Japan was to over-run some 800,000 square miles and plant the ball of blood of its flag over Hong Kong, the Philippines, Thailand (which Mitchell had visited as Siam and had included in his military prophecies), Malaya, the Netherlands East Indies and Burma.

"There is hardly enough time," Mitchell said during his honeymoon and inspection trip, "to crowd in all the work that must be done to give America the greatest air force in the world. There are so many things to learn about the air strategy to come. The globe is shrinking into a small sphere."

Constantly in pursuit of aeronautical knowledge, he had flown not only over the Far East but had crossed Manchuria. He had flown from Berlin to Moscow in twelve hours, then considered somewhat of a record. He had landed at Borodino where Napoleon had spilled blood and where much more was destined to flow. In the land of the Soviets he watched grimly the patient Russians training to fly in suicidal DH-4's with Liberty engines which Russia, with childish trustfulness, had bought with enthusiasm from American producers. Many Russians were killed while training in these "flaming coffins."

This development profoundly disturbed Mitchell who described it later in one of his books. Now, Billy Mitchell's ideas of air power thundered across the country from his charming home at Middleburg, Virginia. "Boxwood," he called it; the restful quarters of a restless host. Here, between inspection trips and his duties as Assistant Chief of the Air Corps, he spun his dreams of the flying age. Here he entertained royally his war comrades, some of whom were frankly dubious of his predictions.

He was a happy man, cocky, self-confident and critical. The controversy raging over his head reminded him of his "joy of combat" in France where he showed marked preference for a fight in the air as against the dull routine of observation and reporting. He laughed over memories of the pink breeches he had worn "for luck," flying over the German lines.

Newspapers of the nation were featuring his exploits with editorial cartoons usually depicting the Army and Navy as huge, fat, slumbering figures being stirred out of pleasant dreams by a swooping Billy Mitchell in a fighting plane.

During this period, the Air Chief's hopes for improvement of the Air Force rose suddenly one afternoon when he received a call from General Pershing who wanted to see him. He hurried off to keep the appointment.

"Perhaps," he said to Farewell Bragg, "the Old Boy is beginning to see the light. Maybe the sinking of the battleships has impressed him at last."

But Mitchell, facing the aging warrior, found Pershing in full regalia, arranging a mass of papers. He wanted to refresh his recollections about the last war, and was fiddling around with material from diaries, newspapers, notebooks. He was talking about writing his memoirs, recalling episodes of the past, the early days, finally the AEF, the "great push" on land, the collapse of Germany. He had to leave soon, he said, to talk at a banquet. In his middle sixties, his fingers trembled a little as he shuffled his documents.

The Air Chief enlightened him on the few points which Pershing proposed to include in his book about the Air Force.

"Are you going to say anything about airplanes being able to sink battleships?" Mitchell inquired.

"No," the General replied coldly. "I'm going to stop with the Armistice. That will cover about everything."

Mitchell was to be mentioned casually, however, in Pershing's story which finally grew into two volumes. The old General was to express some regrets about the state of the American Air Force when the war began: "In looking back over the period immediately prior to our entry ... the very primitive state of our aviation still gives me a feeling of humiliation...

"The failure of our aviation bureau to keep abreast of airplane development in the contending armies cost us serious delay... Colonel Mitchell came to discuss aviation . . . approved recommendations for location of air parks. . . . . . Held conference with Senior Aviation Officers Foulois, W. B. Burt and later Mitchell. Newspaper clippings from home proclaim thousands of American airplanes in France. Have cabled protest... some of the more sensational newspapers at home are making extravagant claims about the large number of American planes actively engaged in France when in fact, up to this moment there is not a single plane of American make on the Western front."

Those fifty-five airplanes, fifty-one of them obsolete and the other four obsolescent with which the United States had entered the war in 1917 were still flying around in Pershing's mind. But the war was over. What had happened to $1,650,000,000 spent for 196 "flaming coffins" was a mystery about which the old General did not propose to speculate. As he arranged his papers for his memoirs America ranked eighth in air power, with Poland seventh, six years after the Armistice.

In air defense, the United States, considering the progress of other nations, was as helpless as Pershing had found it in 1917; worse, perhaps, because ignorance, greed and self-conceit in authority was about to ruin the most air-minded man the country had produced.

7 - THE ORDEAL BEGINS

IN THE YEAR 1925, Billy Mitchell was to learn that it is the cause and not merely the death that makes the martyr. He had long ago counted the inevitable consequence to himself of his attitude, and the hopelessness of his crusade against the ignorance of bureaucrats, among whom the most ignorant were the most violently opposed to him. As he remarked on the eve of the battle which, he was almost certain, would wreck his military career, "Heaven and earth fight in vain against a dunce."

In his darkest hours, for this man had his moments of despair, he often turned to the philosophies of Schiller and Schopenhauer. He had not forgotten Gutzon Borglum's conclusions that there were not in all America five or six men of power or position who cared enough about America to attempt to break the grip of greed which, from the time of the first World War, had been choking our national defense by ruining all our prospects of air power.

But Borglum had not counted on Mitchell. Students of aviation history in years to come may wonder how one man, like flint that would not melt, could have found the time and the energy to fight, under almost daily blows, to arouse in the nation a sense of apprehension of the future. Basically, Mitchell clung to two purposes up to the time of his death: the first, to establish America as a nation protected by the largest air force in the world under a single head; and, the second, to end the folly of spending millions of dollars for battleships which, in the next war, would only rule the seas when the planes on their side ruled the skies above them.

His conclusions were to be proved to the hilt in a terrified world less than six headlong years after his death, and his efforts to save his country were, finally, to break his heart and cut him off just at the time that his usefulness to that country would have been incalculable. Mitchell knew there was but one thing to do: to speak out with a courage that rose from a sense of duty. His fateful year had hardly reached its second month when he charged in a public address as Assistant Chief of the Army Air Service that the Navy was deliberately concealing the real facts of our air status and that officers who were in a position to tell the truth were intimidated by disciplinary action. His ordeal had begun.

Two days later, he defied his superiors by appearing before a House Aircraft Committee-hearing as an emphatic advocate of his unified Air Service plan. He drew the lightning immediately from the White House which instructed Secretary Weeks to withhold his reappointment pending a satisfactory explanation of his actions.

Newspapers soon carried the report that he might be summarily removed from his post. Weeks wrote a stormy letter to Mitchell's chief, Major General Mason Mathews Patrick demanding an explanation of his assistant's activities which, by this time, had thrown the government, the General Staff and Navy heads into violent agitation.

Patrick, who had frequently expressed his disgust for the vast machinery of evil which had caused the shocking air scandal of the past war, made no effort to calm the situation. He was not a man to mince words, though he managed to keep his post by tempering his statements until he was retired in December of 1927, exhausted and disillusioned. Yet it was Patrick, who, exactly four years previously, had declared in a public address reproduced in the Aeronautical Digest of January 1924, that "the money we wasted [to build aircraft during the last war] would provide for our aviation program for four hundred years!"

He went further with his views in the same issue of the Digest:

"It is possible for aircraft to cross the Atlantic in less than two days. Four Barling bombers can carry bombs equal to the entire amount dropped on London during the last war. The operation of these craft is not limited to the seacoast, but it can extend far into the interior. You can well imagine what a well-equipped bombing force attacking our country could do, were we not in a position to defend ourselves. Against such a possibility we must be prepared to ensure our national safety."

All this from Mitchell's own chief in January 1924, when the steel and rubber lobbies were handling senators and congressmen like salesmen on the road to stock up on more battleships and dirigibles. Eighteen years later, when President Roosevelt was calling frantically for 60,000 airplanes and telling a stunned nation that it could expect air attacks as far west as Chicago from the eastern coast, the taxpaying multitudes were beginning to appreciate the emotions of Rip Van Winkle when he awakened with his rusted flintlock beside him after twenty years of drugged sleep.

While his career was reaching a critical point, the air crusader advocated the use of parachute troops: "A large airship can carry 200 fully equipped infantrymen and drop them off in parachute."

Of his assistant, Major General Patrick said later: "His ego is highly developed, and he has an undoubted love of the limelight, a desire to be in the public eye. He is forceful, aggressive, spectacular.

He has a better knowledge of the tactics of air fighting than any man in this country, and, as has been said, was jubilantly proclaiming the power of aircraft and would lose no opportunity to take a fling at the Navy. I think I understood quite well his characteristics, the good in him, and there was much of it, and his faults."

But Billy Mitchell, slashing away in 1925, was so far ahead of his supporters that he had no time to look back. Almost immediately he was in a tangle with Rear Admiral Moffett, who fought to defend his aeronautics bureau from the flying hero's charges of incompetency. These attacks Moffett accepted as "the mouthings of a rabble rouser" but they were to be proved well-founded by the catastrophes of the dirigibles Shenandoah, the Akron (with the loss of Moffett's own life) and finally the Macon, all part of a ghastly record of failure upon failure with the squandering of millions of dollars.

For days Mitchell appeared before the House Aircraft Committee to widen his assaults upon the government's air policy. The War and Navy departments defended themselves with glib witnesses, ready with masses of statistics, who seemed to impress the congressmen, most of whom looked upon the crusader as an incredible, wild-eyed Jules Verne, a crank, and worse.

Mitchell now resorted to the radio to drive his warnings home, startling New York with the charge that the metropolis would be helpless under air attack. In desperation the War Department went back to 1921 in an attempt to establish an accusation that he had disobeyed orders in the bombings of the German battleship.

Mitchell answered by countering that the Navy, now already obsolete, would be powerless under air assault. He was supported vigorously by Captain Rickenbacker before the Congressional hearings. While the air crackled with charges and counter-charges, the peppery Assistant Chief was never too busy to be human.

It was a fight worthwhile, and his enthusiasm, which always came back stronger after his frustrations, never reached greater heights. He would slap his friends on the back. There was something to live for. In six months, a baby was expected at his house.

"I hope it's a daughter," he said, his face beaming, "Billy Junior needs a sister." (Billy Junior was a son of the General's previous marriage.)

Billy Junior was already having fun sprawling on the floor with airplane models. His father, at home from flying tours of inspection, wrote late into the night page upon page in a flowing, tireless hand, piling up on his desk the manuscript of Winged Defense, a book full of keen perception, renewing his demand for a separate air service and launching into a now unchallengeable denunciation of the air policy of his day.

All this did not keep him from penning innumerable magazine and newspaper articles which he dashed off to support his favorite topic. Friends would find him writing while he munched a sandwich and swallowed cups of black coffee.

Week by week, the presses of the national periodicals were rolling off such articles as "Civil and Commercial Aviation," "Aeronautical Era," "Aircraft Dominates Seacraft," "American Leadership in Aeronautics," "How Should we Organize our Air Power?" all for the Saturday Evening Post, whose far-seeing editor, Horace Lorimer begged for more; "Look Out Below!" for Collier's; altogether, a mass of material which would have filled volumes, read avidly by the millions.

It thrilled the younger generation, which in a little more than fifteen years was to take to the skies to save America and confirm all the predictions he had ever made. By this time the whole country was talking daily of Billy Mitchell.

The House Aircraft Committee, in a state of alarm, asked Secretary Weeks of the War Department and Secretary Wilbur of the Navy Department to send their experts to discuss plans of air defense in secret session.

Again, Mitchell was called before them by the congressmen, and reiterated his accusations of the Administration.

President Coolidge was beginning to lose his temper, and according to one account, after reading some of the magazine articles which he believed should not have been written without his permission, pounded his fist on his desk and labeled Mitchell as a "goddamned disturbing fanatic!"

Weeks and Wilbur were urging the President to rebuke Mitchell publicly. Weeks had had to appear before the House Committee for interminable questioning, and was tired and becoming ill.

Grossly ignorant of the subject of aircraft, mopping his face and attacking Mitchell personally, he accused him of violating the President's orders by having failed to show him his essays before the public got them.

Mitchell hotly denied he had betrayed his privileges. In a blistering statement he rendered Weeks' charges ridiculous.

It began to appear that the crusader would not be reappointed as Assistant Chief of the Air Service. He had added to his list of opponents the powerful Major General Charles T. Menoher who was tired of being prodded about the air controversy.

"And yet," Mitchell commented, "all I told them was the truth. It's impossible to make them understand their ignorance!"

Mitchell's friends sought to save him. Many urged him to take a vacation to cool off. He was almost persuaded to leave his battle-ground, and for a time contemplated a photographic aerial expedition to British East Africa.

"I might find some intelligent people there," he said sarcastically.

Captain Rickenbacker, well acquainted with the stupidities and machinations of the army clique, offered him a lucrative post in the Rickenbacker Motor Company. Mitchell squeezed his old friend's arm in gratitude but turned the job down.

"I'm not out until I'm counted out," he said. "If the only thing I can contribute to this fight is my resignation, I might as well call myself a betrayer of the American people. I created this situation and I'm in it to the finish!"

Of interest during the present days of supercharged enthusiasm for the airplane is Mitchell's criticism of the weakness and incompetence of the Philippine and Hawaiian air defenses, already referred to, and which was to be the first warning on the records of congress of the cataclysm to come. No official attention was given to these observations and Mitchell was castigated as usual by his enemies as a warmonger.

Nevertheless, he attended on the evening of the day of these declarations, with the demeanor of an accredited diplomat a reception at the White House where, with a disarming smile, maybe more of a grin, he extended his hand to Coolidge, who, with a look of pain, slid his own frigid digits out of a stiff cuff and quickly turned to the next guest in line.

"How much of what he says does Billy Mitchell really believe himself?" his friends asked in bewilderment. To most of them he had become rather like the picador in an arena, irritating the bull with no intention of wounding him seriously.

But the bull was snorting with rage, his actions thoroughly predictable. There was hardly a breathing spell between the proddings of Mitchell's lance. Repercussions were being heard from the Philippines which, he insisted, could be completely subjugated by air attacks. The Navy hurried Rear Admiral H. P. Jones to the House Aircraft Committee to deny these hallucinations. Former Army and Navy pilots of the last war gathered to endorse Mitchell's contentions and upheld his views in telegrams to the President.

Mitchell derided the Navy's bombing tests on the battleship Washington, an abortive demonstration carefully calculated, he was convinced, to undermine his theory of aircraft and sea craft.

He offered to sink the North Dakota before the entire House Aircraft Committee which by this time had reached a state of exhaustion. Meanwhile, a strong supporter from an unexpected quarter had put in an appearance to defend Mitchell and add to the consternation of the big Navy bureaucrats.

Rear Admiral Sims suddenly announced his conviction that the airplane had made the battleship obsolete. This authority, who had been chief of all-American Naval operations in European waters in the first World War could not be laughed out of court. He spoke with the experience and knowledge of a great fleet commander and expert in sea warfare.

His statement had the effect of throwing the Naval War College into a state of bewilderment from which it did not emerge until the Japanese had demonstrated the devastating truth of it sixteen years later.

The press of the nation rang with the controversy. Billy Mitchell had stirred an interest, the extent of which had not been experienced in this country since the Monitor met the Merrimac. His predictions were debated from the cracker-barrel assembly of the country stores to the club lounges of the metropolitan rich. Coolidge, studying the editorials, listening to the protests of his cabinet, had by this time, heard enough. Among his intimates his views on the subject of the airplane were well known.

"Flying machines" were still in a state of infancy and would so remain if he had to decide what to do about them. The wheel was still a pretty good invention.

Early in March of 1925, the President called Secretary Weeks to the White House and told him what he proposed to do about "that buzzard." Weeks, in complete agreement, conferred at once with Major General John L. Hines, his chief of staff and Major General Patrick who reluctantly accepted the President's decision.

According to a well-informed source of the period, Coolidge had told Weeks: "Mitchell will have to keep his mouth shut from now on or he will be penalized until he learns his lesson. He has talked more in the past three months than I have since I was born!"

The public was stunned with the news that Mitchell had been reduced to his regular army grade of Colonel and ordered to Texas as air officer of the Eighth Corps Area. He received the blow while denouncing to the press what had proved to be a lamentable demonstration of anti-aircraft artillery at Fortress Monroe.

He appeared prepared for his demotion, though his comments to friends clearly indicated the distress he felt about leaving "Boxwood" and his Southern companions. At any rate he hoped his baby would be born in Virginia, his favorite state. "You may tell the people," he added, to the reporters, "that I will continue my fight for a Unified Air Service!"

He renewed his defiance on the eve of his departure at a luncheon in his honor at the Army and Navy Club in Washington. There were a few days left

before his exile to Texas where he was to be cruelly disciplined without command. Piles of newspapers, their headlines blaring the facts of his demotion, were stacked unread in his study where a few privileged intimates were permitted to drop in for a handshake. He was hard at work again, his light burning into the small hours of the morning. His book Winged Defense had to be finished.

Tired, weary-eyed, he drove his pen across the pages.

"The brass heads of the General Staff," he said, "will find this hard to swallow, but by God, it's the truth as I know it! The people must be told."

His written words of 1925 sound today as an inspiration while our air program is approaching 60,000 machines a year and Britain in one night sends 1,000 airplanes to bombard Hitlerite Germany. No one but Billy Mitchell is on record seventeen years ago as having even vaguely visualized this.

'Winged Defense' was all on paper at long last, and the soldier author, wiping his forehead, read his greatest predictions with the satisfaction of a prophet who believed in his message with a burning, unquenchable faith.

His words will engrave themselves upon the tablets of history. They were written on "the threshold of the aeronautical era," as he described it and which he saw as clearly as the rays of the rising sun which was now pouring through his lattice upon his finished manuscript.

Read the words which now shine through the gloom of our times; warnings as ominous when they were written as they were true. They meant nothing to a blind nation in 1925:

"During this epoch the destinies of all people will be controlled through the air."

"A country should have the necessary air forces always ready at the outbreak of war, because this is the story of our arms that will enter into combat, and it is upon a favorable air decision that the whole fate of a war may depend."

"The time will come when the transportation of large bodies of troops across the ocean by seacraft will be completely impossible."

"The only effective defense against aerial attack is to whip the enemy's air forces in air battles."

"If a nation ambitious for universal conquest gets off to a flying start in a war of the future it may be able to control the whole world more easily than a nation has controlled a continent in the past."

8 - EXILE

THE SPRING OF 1925 FOUND BILLY MITCHELL in the uniform of a colonel, pacing a barren office in the dull obscurity of Fort Sam Houston at San Antonio. His face already was becoming that of the true reformer biding his time before the open assault to uproot a system he knows to be evil. The General's exile could not have been better calculated to increase his mental torture. His superiors at the Fort had informed him coldly that no instructions had been received from the War Department to assign him to a command. In a few days he was as restless as a caged animal.

The daily routine never varied. Hanging up his hat and coat, sitting at a desk, studying innocuous papers and fiddling with them until lunchtime when, more by respect than force of habit, the men at his post, down to the servants, addressed him as a general: "Take this chair, General." "Another cup of coffee, General?"

One event of the upheaval had pleased Mitchell. He had been succeeded as Assistant Chief of the Air Service by Lieutenant Colonel James E. Fechet, who had been identified with the Air Service since 1917. Fechet was heartily in sympathy with Mitchell's views but was inclined to the belief that conditions would "eventually straighten themselves out."

Promoted through the grades, now in the post from which his superior had been removed he was to climb to the top as Chief of the Air Corps with the rank of major general within two years.

"Fechet is a good man," Mitchell said, when a month later his successor had become a brigadier general. "He's of the Army of the Line. He believes as I do. He'll do his job, but I'll do the talking."

Reminded of these days a decade later, Billy Mitchell admitted that the full realization of the effect on the country of his crusade had not yet dawned fully in his mind. The Wisconsin assembly had hailed his revelations as an inspiration to the nation's patriotism and soon he was invited to become a candidate for congress by an enthusiastic group in Milwaukee where he went to renew his attack on the military bureaucracy in a sulphurous address.

Josephus Daniels, former Secretary of the Navy, who had vigorously protested Mitchell's unauthorized campaign for a Unified Air Service in a caustic correspondence in 1920 with Newton D. Baker, then Secretary of War, and had even demanded the muzzling of the crusader, now, in a flag-waving speech in Cleveland, lauded the demoted brigadier general as a messiah.

Mitchell laughed grimly over the national repercussions which followed his banishment.

"One thing is certain," he remarked. "I'm not going into politics to fight this thing out. The politicians, from the White House down, are responsible for this whole tragic mess. What chance would I have if I became one of them! The people will believe me if I want nothing from them."

Though grounded in San Antonio in self-defense by his superiors who feared him, Mitchell's predictions and warnings were like a stone flung into a vast lake whose ripples were inexorably widening, to reach during the coming years into every channel of modern defense. The world was to remember his prophecies, and trace their implications into the future. The vindication to come to him was to be the usual reward civilization bestows upon such men—after making sure that they are dead.

As the dreary months dragged by in Texas, the exile fell back upon his "saving anchor," as he called it; his articles, which he proceeded to work at with a recaptured enthusiasm.

Again, the magazine presses began to distribute his message to every corner of the land: "Aircraft in the National Defense," "Building a Futile Navy," "Russian Aeronautics," "When Air Raiders Come," and so forth.

In Washington, the General Staff read these blasts and fumed. What could be done to gag this revolutionary fanatic who was undermining the traditions laid down by Von Clausewitz and Mahan?

[Military strategists: Germany's Carl von Clausewitz, 1810-1831; and American naval officer Alfred Thayer Mahan, 1840-1914.]

Mitchell was touched deeply one day when a withered old Texan, whose glittering gimlet eyes belied his age, walked in to shake hands. He was, Mitchell always insisted, the only surviving son of Sam Houston, who had carved out an entire state for his country.

"Old San Jacinto" had loved and labored for Texas, and had died as an unforgettable hero in America's history, leaving nothing to his wife and eight children but a log house, a patch of land and a few loving admonitions from a government which forgot him as soon as the sod blanketed his coffin.

"Fight it out, General!" Sam Houston's descendant stormed, pounding his cane. "You've got a worst gang against you than my father had when he tackled Clay, Webster and the Whigs. For Christ's sake take the advice Andrew Jackson gave my old man in Spanish Florida: 'Get out of your trap and drive out the sons-of-bitches!' "

Perhaps this admonition had some effect on Mitchell, who, after a period of silence was soon lashing out in the press against the forces of reaction entrenched in Washington. Secretary Wilbur had announced an air-training plan to appease those calling for action. Mitchell termed the program "plain bunk." He called Rear Admiral C. F. Hughes' report on anti-aircraft tests "unadulterated bunk." He ridiculed the anti-aircraft demonstrations at Fort Tilden and set up a new clamor for his pet project of a Unified Air Service.

It became the important routine of Texas editors to assign reporters to Colonel Billy Mitchell's office and they rarely returned without a front page "screamer."

One day he exploded a story that made the nation gasp. He had prepared the plans for a non-stop flight from New York to Paris of a super-airplane with a ton of explosives aboard to prove that a loaded bomber could cross the ocean.

The War Department had turned the project down in horror. The air crusader was again taking events in his stride. His book, Winged Defense had been published, to be read behind locked doors and discussed in secret conferences by every official of the War Department. As a matter of fact, it was soon being studied by the governments of all the great powers. The author, meanwhile, literally was pouring into Congress a series of recommendations to be used as measures to remedy the conditions of the sagging Air Force. On August 3, an expected event occurred which he considered almost as important as his crusade: Lucy Trumbull Mitchell was born, the daughter he had hoped for to play with Billy Junior.

So, the months dragged on, the prisoner filing at his chains. On a soft, cheerful day in early September Mitchell sat in his small quarters watching the sky which had turned into a fountain of color. He loved the sun, and from boyhood looked up at it with childlike confidence. Skyways, the title of one of his books, was to be inspired much later by such daydreaming.

His mind continually associated the heavens with the wings of man, but now it toyed with an impulse which was to put his courage and integrity to the rack, and which was to mark a violent turning point in his life. His own words, as spoken to one of the authors of this book, ten years later, describe his motives for an act that has remained ever since a point of debate whenever army officers gather and mention his name.

Few men in Mitchell's position would have done what he dared to do. For three days he had been searching his soul for an answer to the gravest question an army man can face:

Should a soldier, sworn to discipline, condemn and defy his superiors by telling the truth? His own account of his decision speaks for itself:

"I knew the time had come for me to stand as one man against my fellows in a profession to which I had devoted my life. The General Staff, I felt certain, would keep me in my godforsaken post at San Antonio until I had been beaten into submission. I was waiting for an opportunity to seize upon with force and persistence, and crowd it to the utmost, if necessary, to shake the country into a realization of its danger. I was turning over in my mind a statement for the press on the loss in the Pacific of the PN-9 No. 1 which, I had been informed, had been sent on a suicidal flight toward Hawaii without enough gasoline.

"Visions of the 'flaming coffins' flashed through my mind, the stupidities of the Air Service which sent brave men to die and muzzled experienced flyers who knew the truth. There would be no hope for the country until such imbecility, and worse, had been blasted from the scene of national defense.

"I remember the telephone rang as I sat there, and I was stupefied to learn that our dirigible, the Shenandoah, had been totally wrecked in Ohio in a flight from Lakehurst with thirteen of its crew and the loss of its commander. A newspaper wanted a statement from me which I agreed to prepare. The time had come for it. "I soon had the facts from my own sources of information over the long-distance telephone and from press association dispatches. Some of those who helped me to gather the details were well informed, experienced men, ready to risk their own positions to let the country know the truth. The ghastly story was soon unfolded to me.

"The Navy had been in the habit of sending our dirigibles into the country for advertising purposes to make the public feel that something was being done about our air program. In the case of the Shenandoah, it had been ordered to cruise in the middle of the country, from county to county, over our county fairs whose managers wanted to attract crowds and who urged their Congressmen to send the dirigibles along. Congressmen who saw goodwill and plenty of votes behind the requests had found it easy to win the Navy's approval.

"It was a suicidal venture, authorized by dangerous idiots in power who had never traveled in dirigibles or airplanes. The

Shenandoah was sent off from Lakehurst, NJ, under Commander Zachary Landsdowne who could not refuse the order without handing in his resignation. He knew how dangerous his trip was to be. He and his men had to risk the sacrifice of their lives for the whims of a handful of politicians. The airship was sent across the country without any meteorological survey, or scheme of handling it, regardless of the weather.

"Without any reports whatever of the elements, Landsdowne, by his insane murderers in Washington, was ordered by telegram and telephone from place to place, to leave at certain times, as on a train schedule, regardless of the uncertainties of the weather ahead; and this with a dirigible constantly at the mercy of the winds!

"A brave man sworn to obey, Landsdowne flew on, ran into a line squall in the mountains and his helpless ship, with more than half of its safety valves useless, its cells filled with helium, which had been substituted for hydrogen for which she had been originally designed, broke into three distinct pieces in the storm high above Ava, Ohio. The airship was destitute of the parachutes which I had recommended to Admiral Moffett. The vital matter of valves to release gas quickly to enable such a ship to ascend beyond air pressure heights had been totally ignored. Ten of the original eighteen safety valves had been shut off from operation.

"Well, that was the story, and, as I knew those ships as well as I knew that no one would speak out, I would have betrayed my country had I not accused those directly responsible. The disaster was due absolutely to the culpability of the Navy Department. In preparing my conclusions I could find no words strong enough in the English language to express my fury. As a soldier I hated unnecessary loss of life, particularly when at the hands of the stupid and ignorant. I god-damned the gang responsible for the outrage. I was fully aware of the consequences when I announced for publication as a result of this latest outrage piled on top of cumulative stupidities:

"'The high command of both the Army and the Navy are guilty of incompetency, criminal negligence and almost treasonable administration of the national defense.'"

Billy Mitchell's charges, shouted in headlines across the land, stirred the nation to profound depths. The Teapot Dome scandal was still in the air, and Coolidge, agitated by the tumult until he actually trembled with rage, according to a member of his own Cabinet, ordered Dwight F. Davis, acting Secretary of War to recognize Mitchell's attack by immediate action. Davis' superior, Secretary Weeks, one of Harding's "back to normalcy" boosters, a Massachusetts Old Guard Republican who believed in keeping both feet on the ground, had been driven to his bed during this excitement. He died ten months later, never having changed his conviction that Mitchell was a dangerous opportunist, a "man on horseback," a Boulanger, who would eventually land in an insane asylum if Coolidge knew his way about.

Meanwhile, Secretary Wilbur, of the Navy, sealed his lips. He refused to utter a word about the affair, now fanned into agitating headlines by a Congressional clamor to promote Mitchell immediately. The crusader added to the outcry by renewing his demands, from his sunbaked post at San Antonio, for an Aeronautics Bureau under a Secretary of Air. Admiral Moffett, under whose department the Shenandoah had been operating, went about drawn and white-faced, actually cursing the demoted Air Chief: "I wish he was in hell!"

One may go back to Herbert Spencer, a favorite of Mitchell's bookshelf, to illuminate the subject of the responsibility he assumed when he branded his superiors as dealers in treason. Mitchell quoted Spencer's following paragraph often enough, carrying a copy of it in his pocket, reading it aloud and punctuating it with eleven blunt words: "That explains me to myself and to those who will understand."

WHOEVER HESITATES TO UTTER THAT which he thinks the highest truth, lest it should be too much in advance of the time, may reassure himself by looking at his acts from an impersonal point of view. Let him duly realize the fact that opinion is the agency through which character adapts external arrangements to itself—that his opinion rightly forms part of this agency—is a unit of force, constituting, with other such units, the general power which works out social changes, and he will perceive that he may properly give full utterance to his innermost conviction, leaving it to produce what effect it may.

It is not for nothing that he has in him these sympathies with some principles and repugnance to others. He, with all his capacities and beliefs, is not an accident, but a product of the time. He must remember that while he is a descendant of the past, he is a parent of the future, and that his thoughts are as children born to him, which he may not carelessly let die. Not as adventitious therefore will the wise man regard the faith which is in him. The highest truth he sees he will fearlessly utter. Knowing that, let what may come of it, he is thus playing his right part in the world—knowing that if he can affect the change he aims at—well; if not—well also; though not so well.

It was to be "not so well" for Billy Mitchell. He reviewed the story, over and over again, before a handful of disciples, most of whom quoted it as it is written down here from his own lips:

"While the Army clique was hesitating to try me, during the tumult of the press and the outcries of Congress, I felt as a fighter must feel in the ring when he has his opponent on the ropes. Now was the time for the knockout. I confess now that I would have liked the job of Air Chief of the USA.

"What an opportunity to throttle the Air Trust, to scrap the damned 'flaming coffins,' to provide our men with safe training planes, to direct a Bureau of Aeronautics with a vast laboratory to prepare for the future War of the Air!

"The controversy had resulted in the usual action taken by power politics under fire: investigations, boards of inquiry, announcements that something would be done, all to quiet the public.

"Nothing would ever come of these performances but whitewashings, pigeon-holing of reports whose revelations, usually heard in secret might upset the status quo, but yet the fact that bodies of elected representatives were holding hearings, asking questions, subpoenaing witnesses was a sign that the people whose lives were involved, were becoming too voluble to be ignored. They were beginning to think and assert themselves. Democracy moves slowly.

"News reached me that Dwight Davis would take full responsibility for any discipline to be imposed on me. He favored an air inquiry by an impartial agency and undoubtedly influenced Coolidge to appoint the so-called Morrow Board for the purpose, a recommendation I had urged for many months, but not the horse-and-buggy personnel with which it emerged.

"Senator Couzens called for a full investigation of my charges, but Secretary Wilbur, practically in hiding from the press, opposed further airings. He attended dinner parties, sitting with his head in his hands, murmuring: 'Let it die! Let it die!' Reluctant to enter the picture, at the last minute he announced he would help an inquiry if one was ordered.

"Departments of the American Legion were stirring the country with resolutions demanding a separate Air Service. Representative Lampert, whose committee had done much to bring the whole air issue to the surface, supported me. Meanwhile, Coolidge, in hushed conferences with Secretary Davis began to insert his cold hand into the proceedings. He wanted me to be tried by a court-martial solely on the issue of discipline.

"The truth of my disclosures were to have nothing to do with the action to be taken against me. Representative W. A. Oldfield pledged the Democratic support of the Congress to my cause, but I was trying desperately to avoid a political battle which would have ground my issue to pieces between the millstones of the two opposing parties.

"Congressman LaGuardia rushed in to join my recruits, offering his services in my defense. Mayor J. M. Curley of Boston satisfied his passion for headlines by backing me "to the death"—his or mine, I was then too much occupied to figure out which. The formalities of the inquisition began. I was asked to make a formal admission of my charges to Major General E. Hinds, which I agreed to, readily enough. Admiral Moffett attacked me venomously in the press in an effort to defend his own incompetency.

"Senator Wadsworth of New York added to the commotion by suggesting an airplane flight from New York to Peking, an idea which must have developed from one of his Homeric feasts. I was told I would have an opportunity of appearing before Coolidge's Board of Inquiry on the aircraft situation. Wilbur and Davis were issuing statements almost daily."

"Reports were flying about that I was to be put under arrest when, as September was coming to an end, I was relieved from active duty, as it was laughingly described, under the orders of General Hinds. It was by that time well known in Army circles that Coolidge had taken over the responsibility of having me tried under charges of violating the Ninety-sixth Article of War, involving discipline—and limited to discipline.

"He proposed to review the findings himself. Nevertheless, I flew about the country collecting evidence to prove the downtrodden condition of the Air Service. I knew what it felt then to be the headline of the day, smothered by reporters, blinded by photographers. I hope the thousands of youngsters who crowded about me then, clamoring for autographs on their model planes, will appreciate what it all meant when war comes again."

BILLY MITCHELL ARRIVED IN WASHINGTON from St. Louis on September 24 with 800 pounds of papers consisting of the evidence he proposed to present. He was greeted as a conquering hero by a tumultuous, flag-waving crowd of American Legionnaires, who hoisted him to their shoulders over his protests and struggles. Soon he had the almost delirious veterans under control, after a fashion, and succeeded in quelling what threatened to develop into a menacing outburst of bitter defiance when the greeters discovered that the police had interfered with their plans for a triumphant parade with banners and torch lights to the doors of the White House.

The flyer's supporters appeased themselves more or less a day later by dragging the demoted General to a fabulous barbecue where he was the honored guest, sitting like an Indian Chief in the center of a crowded circle of cheering men who had seen war with him.

"Speech, General, speech!" they yelled. "They can't pull you down! We won't let them! We know what you did. We know you're right!"

But Mitchell waved off the demands, smiling, though his eyes were wet. He munched in silence. Again, he sprang into the headlines with a scathing denunciation of Army aviation in a 3,500-word statement before the latest Air Board inquiry. Publicly he lamented the lost Hawaiian flyers of the PN-9.

Facing an investigative body, he struck at the "haphazard methods of the Shenandoah flight," of the fatal Hawaiian hop, and even of the Macmillan polar expedition.

The War Department was issuing statistics to upset the figures he had included in his arguments when it received word that the President was becoming impatient. Mitchell had been holding the front pages of the nation for days. Coolidge's favorite Springfield Republican and the usually placid Hartford Courant actually were blowing the General's trumpet. According to a White House secretary, the headlines provoked the usually silent Coolidge to stab his grapefruit in the morning as though spearing a fish through the ice. Often, he muttered a conservative "Damn!" Occasionally, after he had cautiously peered about, a ringing "God damn!"

"Push the button!" the President shouted to Secretary Davis over the telephone. "He'll drive the country into hysterics. Put him on trial where he'll have to answer 'yes' or 'no,' two short words with which he will now become acquainted!"

Mitchell almost immediately received a copy of the charges for which he was to face a court-martial. Friends with him at the time remember that his face reddened as he read the accusations. Not a loophole was included in them to permit him to explain the motives behind his years of constructive criticism in his country's cause. The particulars might well have been served on some dazed and ignorant second lieutenant.

Billy's anger may have influenced his open defiance on the next day when he issued a public plea to the American Legion to support by national action a Unified Air Service. It was his old battle cry, which may even yet penetrate Washington's ears:

"The time has come when we must modernize our national defense, teach our people what it means, and organize it in a simple, direct and efficient manner. This can be brought about by creating a Department of National Defense, with subheads for the Air, the Army and the Navy. It is one of the broadest questions before this country today. In the interest of economy and efficiency it is not a question of persons or a question of political party. It is one which concerns the national security of this greatest of all Nations. The American Legion is the institution which should initiate the movement and show the people that this is the best organization for defense. My best regards to you all."

The appeal received national publicity. At his breakfast table Coolidge read the news as a slap in the face. He considered the statement as a direct violation of his recently expressed wishes to discourage the use of propaganda in any form by the members of the armed services. Now the President, with the cold relentlessness of an angered Vermonter, rasped out his orders for the inquisition. He appointed Davis with full authority as Secretary of War. According to well-founded reports the Chief Executive had induced Weeks, now completely incapacitated, to resign and sent him friendly admonitions to "relax."

During this period, little but Mitchell was talked about at Coolidge's Cabinet meetings. Would a court-martial shut up this man? Weeks had once described him as "charging around like a goat let loose." Benedict M. Holden, the Connecticut lawyer and politician, who spent a night with Coolidge at the White House, at this time, serves again as authority for the following classical remark Coolidge is said to have made about Mitchell as he prepared to retire after a hard day, "In New England," cried the President in irritation, while in weariness he pulled off the Congress gaiters he had not yet discarded for low shoes, "we would call that man an unprincipled horse-trader."

While Coolidge was agitated almost to despair by the tremendous volume of space devoted by the press to Billy Mitchell's campaign, he could not have found much cause for irritation in the editorials about the excitement.

Powerful newspapers, daily setting aside front-page space under large headlines for the controversy were far from ready to accept

Mitchell's predictions. Influential publishers believed in large battle-ships, which kept the great steel mills humming. Editorial writers at this critical point of Mitchell's career were soon calling him a loud-mouthed visionary. The New York Times gave him a rough dusting of the jacket following his denunciation of the High Command. Its front page, however, considered him the most important man of the day.

And yet it was the Times which had said editorially on May 2, 1918 under a heading "A Federal Grand Jury for the Airplane in-quiry," when the billion-dollar aircraft scandal was beginning to muddy the waters: "These conditions plainly point to an organized conspiracy, bold, powerful, and numerous; made up of men able to formulate a great and definite plan and embracing within their num-ber men sufficiently high placed and influential to have the ear and the confidence of the Secretary of War."

All this was forgotten now, although the "men sufficiently high placed" were still conspiring; this time to ruin Mitchell at all cost; to cast him out. The Air Trust had never slept since 1917, and with the help of its confederates in the government was to thwart the cru-sader until his death. His revelations and his prophecies, however, as far back as 1920 had made him an international figure.

In Europe, aviation chiefs of all-important nations were quietly studying every prediction he made, while frivolous and popular pa-pers in England and France ridiculed his theories. Using, as an example, the disastrous earthquake in Japan, which had caused a loss of $50,000,000 in property damage on May 23, 1925, Mitchell warned the world that the first air raid in the war to come would be even more intense than the Japanese catastrophe. [The 6.8 Kita Tajima earth-quake which caused 272 deaths.]

He was laughed at openly for this prediction. He aroused a storm of criticism in the British Isles with the statement that an at-tack by 1,000 planes from England could be made upon the United States, as far as the Middle West.

The international prominence given to this theory gravely dis-turbed Coolidge, who lived in constant fear that such talk might arouse national suspicion and hatred and bring about an armament race. It was with obvious satisfaction sometime later that he passed around to his Cabinet a clipping of an editorial entitled "Bogeys and Madmen" from the London Daily News, whose editors, deriding Mitchell, were as incredulous as most Americans were, for years to come, of the crusader's staggering warnings of doom.

9 - THE TORCH AND THE FAGOTS

A CROWD LARGE ENOUGH TO POPULATE A town was gathered early in the morning in front of the gloomy structure known as the Emory Building, at the foot of Capitol Hill in Washington on October 28, 1925. Men and women, many of them holding children in their arms, craned their necks, peering down the street. Irritable policemen occasionally pushed them back when it appeared the entrance to the building might be blocked.

Built in the distant past, the dilapidated edifice was one of Washington's battered landmarks, and only the oldest inhabitants of the capital could give a vague idea of when it was new. Some said it was falling apart. It first housed the Census Bureau for many years, was vacant for almost a generation, only to be rehabilitated during the first World War as a commissary. Now it was used by the War Department to preserve forgotten and musty military records, all in a confused mass, packed in crates and barrels.

Inside, the cracked plastered walls of this warehouse dripped with dampness. In this place was the "courtroom" where Billy Mitchell was to be tried. In selecting it, the War Department bureaucrats were certainly not dignifying either themselves or the trial which was to be held in it.

To the excited assembly outside, the occasion had touches of an old-time public hanging. Words passed about, while men looked up from their newspapers which they were eagerly scanning for the latest details. But the crowd was with Billy Mitchell, now under technical arrest, his movements restricted to the city. He was compelled even to telephone his whereabouts to the War Department from public restaurants.

High officers were filing into the courthouse, stern of demeanor, in uniforms which clinked with decorations, and their hands on their swords. Generals, some of them red-faced and important, others sad and worried-looking, came hurrying through the door.

The military inquisitors were said to be the highest-ranking court-martial in personnel ever convened in the United States, more imposing, even, than the French officers who had sent Dreyfus to Devil's Island.

With one exception they were all West Pointers, set to try this upstart who had only come from the Army of the Line. No officer of the Air Service was on the board, two general officers of that branch having been ruled out as ineligible on account of their own intimate concern in the public charges which Mitchell had flung at the High Command. Some said that no one on the court-martial board had ever even been in an airplane. While the trial generals were composing themselves in an inside room, arranging their tangled medals, perhaps, and nodding imperiously to each other, a great cheer burst from the street. Billy Mitchell, accompanied by his wife, was pushing and struggling through the dense crowd which had recognized him with a spontaneous, uproarious shout and now blocked his progress.

He was in full uniform, his breast covered with his service ribbons. He carried a bamboo cane, and, somehow through the press on the steps of the courthouse, he managed to release his arm and wave his stick in the air as a sword above a hurricane of gestures and cries, little fluttering flags and adoring faces.

"It's for America," he shouted. "The truth must come out!"

An ocean of words was to be written of this famous trial, to be forgotten until dreadnaughts were sunk from the sky and people cowered in bomb shelters. The record of the court-martial alone was to consist of 1,400,000 words, enough for seven thick volumes, but apparently not enough to convince the United States that one American against the world, one patriot who had pledged himself to risk and struggle and responsibility and, yes, even disgrace, had actually and in truth stripped a curtain from the future.

One development interested Billy Mitchell above the many which followed as his trial opened. The judge advocates which President Coolidge had recommended to try him had been replaced suddenly by Major Allen Wyant Gullion, assistant trial judge advocate and Colonel Sherman Moreland, judge advocate of the Fifth Corps Area at Columbus, Ohio, who had been selected with less regard for his knowledge of aviation than for his supposed powers of invective, as the crowded hall was to discover.

After the trial, when the information was to prove of little use but to strengthen his conviction that the Air Trust had an arm reaching into the government, Mitchell learned that the specifications of accusations had been served upon him by an officer of the War Department who had been named in an ugly connection in a classic plea for an investigation of the aircraft monopoly on January 29, 1924. On his death bed in 1936, Billy Mitchell, who had never forgotten the ordeal of his trial, told one of the authors of this book: "Look up the files of the first session of the Sixty-Eighth Congress for 1924 and you will find a speech by Congressman John M. Nelson of Wisconsin which refers to a Lieutenant Colonel McMullin, a judge advocate. I think he was the one who served the papers on me. He certainly was the right man for the job." [John Mandt Nelson (1870-1955), member of the U.S. House of Representatives for Wisconsin's 2nd district, 1913-1919.]

The authors, in 1942, found the reference which follows, with McMullin's name in a yellowed copy of the Congressional Record:

Mr. Nelson of Wisconsin ...

"...the American people have been lied to ... the cross-license agreement, designed by the Air Trust as its means of controlling the United States Air Service contracts, is still in effect in current contracts and is still the means by which the same Air Trust controls contracts of the United States Air Service. In this connection I desire to note that Colonel Jesse G. Vincent, now a director of the aircraft combination and who during the war was chief engineer in charge of both motor and airplane designs for the Army, is also at this time a stockholder and vice president of the Packard Motor Car Company, which is the recipient of numerous contracts, as I have before noted.

"Mr. Hughes declared in his report (of the billion-dollar Air Trust scandal) that Colonel Vincent's simultaneous connection with the Army and the Packard Motor Car Co., was a violation of the criminal statutes. The War Department, however, did nothing; the Department of Justice did nothing; and we now find that this Colonel Vincent's company still receiving contracts from the Air Service running into millions of dollars in spite of all these things.

"In 1924 we find this company getting contracts. Now, what else did this Air Trust, formed by these inexperienced and incompetent aircraft manufacturers to grab the profits arising from this country's necessities in its hour of dire peril, invent to further throttle independent, experienced, competent, thoroughly established engineers and manufacturers? I shall read again to you from an aircraft corporation contract of April 27, 1923, contract No. 640. I shall read section 2 of that clause of the contract dealing with patent and copyright infringements:

The government will, without limitation to the time of completion of this contract in other respects, hold and save the contractor harmless from all demands and liabilities for alleged use of any copyrighted composition? Patented or unpatented invention, secret process or suggestion in, or in making or supplying, the articles of work herein contracted for, and for alleged use of any copyrighted composition or patented invention in using such articles or work for the purpose for which they are made or supplied, where the demand or liability is based on copyrights or patents that are not owned or controlled by or under which lights are not enjoyed by the contractor ...

... or is based on patents that are not enjoyed by the Manufacturers' Aircraft Association, or patents or rights that are not cross-licensed, under the said cross-license agreement or any supplements thereto; provided immediate notice of any such demand or liability and of any legal proceedings connected therewith is given in writing by the contractor to the contracting officer (the government); and provided further, that the government may intervene in any such demand or proceeding and in its discretion may defend the same or make settlement thereof, and the contractor shall furnish all information in its possession and all assistance of its employees requested by the government.

"The clause I have just read, gentlemen of the House, is what is known as the 'save harmless' clause. This clause will be found in many, if not all, of the contracts contained in the list I have already read into the 'Record.' On the margin of the contract horn which I am quoting, written in longhand, is the following notation: "'approved as to patent clause by direction of the secretary of war,' 'JOS. I. McMullin, Lieutenant Colonel, J.A., May 31, 1923.' The 'save harmless clause' is in fact simply an authority granted by officials of the United States to certain private aircraft manufacturers to steal boldly and deliberately the patents of any inventor whose patent appliances the air trust may desire to use or may find necessary in its continued hold on the government's pocketbook!"

It would appear from a careful study of Representative Nelson's remarks, as quoted above, that there were more skeletons behind the Mitchell trial than President Coolidge cared to reveal. The truth of the "save harmless clause" alone, and its destructive effect upon scores of brilliant airplane inventors, whose patented inventions had been appropriated by the Air Trust, with government approval, would have shocked the nation. Mitchell was completely familiar with the operations of this "legal" piracy. If he had been permitted to lift the lid from this cauldron, some of its steaming slime would have been seen to besmirch some of the greatest industries of the nation operating under the vicious patent-pooling arrangement, which was not confined to the so-called Air Trust.

The cover of this mess was to be only partly pried off in 1942 when our trusting but indifferent public read that "Big Business," through cartels or other arrangements, was dealing with Germany and Japan even after Pearl Harbor, while many of Hitler's tanks were rumbling along on synthetic rubber made by an exclusive American process, according to the testimony of Assistant Attorney General Thurman Arnold. It was not surprising that the Coolidge administration saw to it that Mitchell's court-martial should close the door to any issue but that of discipline and insubordination. Who was this man who believed that, single handed, he could reveal the truth in court of our pitiful air defense when a billion-dollar aircraft scandal had been rocked to sleep?

But this was no time to take a risk with vulnerable prosecutors. Heavy artillery was needed to hold the battle line to the manufactured issue of insubordination. It may now be understood why Lieutenant Colonel McMullin, disclosed as having put his O.K. on the sinister "save harmless" contract in a bargain between the War Department and one of the most powerful companies of the aircraft monopoly suddenly disappeared from any active participation in the trial. He would have loomed up too large as a target for any shots at patent-pooling and the slumbering aircraft scandal. Some smart War Department desk-holder had looked back into the records.

Billy Mitchell saw at once that the form of the accusation that had been served upon him had been cunningly prepared to prevent the introduction of proof of any charges of incompetency in the Nation's air defense. It was all cut and dried:

"That Colonel Mitchell in making the statement of September 5 did conduct himself to the prejudice of good order ... that he made a statement insubordinate to the administration of the War Department ... that he made a statement highly contemptuous and disrespectful of the administration of the War Department with intent to discredit the same ... that the foregoing referred to the Navy Department... all to the prejudice of good order and military discipline..."

Nothing here about the "good order" of airplanes which were crashing on almost every airfield with faithful Army pilots, adding to the record of the dead sacrificed to bureaucratic incompetency and criminal indifference! The disinterestedness in the status of the air service of the marionettes who tried Mitchell was equaled only by that of Coolidge himself. Yet these generals, some of whom were still studying the military tactics of the war with Mexico, were not at heart intentionally culpable men. They were assembled to carry out the intention of the General Staff, which was to muzzle Mitchell at all costs. With the exception of the then Major General Douglas MacArthur, whose sad experience it was to have to deliberate with such a body, the members of the court were unimaginative, routine men who, after Chateau Thierry and Belleau Wood, had gone back to the studies of the fall of Sedan.

As originally constituted, before three of its members were dismissed unceremoniously on challenges of bias by Billy Mitchell, the court-martial was made up of Major General Charles P. Summerall, commanding the Second Corps Area of New York Harbor (and at this writing complaining about ineffective dim-outs); Major General Robert L. Howze, commanding the Fifth Corps Area at Columbus, Ohio; Major General Fred W. Sladen, Superintendent of the United States Military Academy and who had once been quoted as having remarked that "..no officer was worth the powder to blow him to hell unless he was a West Pointer."

Major General MacArthur, commanding the Sixth Corps Area at Baltimore; Major General William S. Graves, commanding the Sixth Corps Area at Chicago; Major General Benjamin A. Poore, commanding the Seventh Corps Area at Omaha; Brigadier General Albert J. Bowley, commanding Fort Bragg, NC; Brigadier General Edward L. King, commandant of the General Service Schools at Fort Leavenworth; Brigadier General Frank R. McCoy, commanding the Third Infantry Brigade at Fort Sam Houston, Tex.; Brigadier General Edwin B. Winans of Fort Clark, Tex.; Brigadier General George LeR. Irwin, commanding Fort Sill at Oklahoma, and Brigadier General Ewing E. Booth, commandant of the Cavalry School at Fort Riley, Kan.

The three members who were bowled over by the challenges of the defense were Summerall, Sladen and Bowley. Their departure was not to have any effect on the results, as Mitchell grimly observed. Secretary Davis permitted the accused to add Colonel Herbert A. White, a judge advocate in the Army, as his military counsel, a gentleman whose efforts in the case still remain a mystery to those who recall the trial.

The air crusader had retained as his chief counsel of defense, Congressman Frank R. Reid of Illinois whose tenaciousness and courage in the battle was to attract the Nation's attention, even the grudgingly expressed admiration of the bitter generals ruling the court. Colonel Blanton Winship stationed at the headquarters of the First Corps Area at Boston, who had done notable work with the Citizens' Military Training Camps, had been appointed law officer, the only member not subject to challenge. As a participant in the ordeal he would be remembered as one of the few men on the Board whose sense of decency prompted him to be fair.

No stronger evidence could have been found of the General Staff's tactics than the attitude of Brigadier General Bowley. Four days before the trial he had made a speech in Greenville, NC, "expressing opinions openly hostile to Mitchell," as one paper had mildly recorded it. As a matter of fact, he had referred inferentially to Mitchell as a "mountebank." He had been hissed during his address, which was made before an American Legion convention. The War Department, well aware of this, had, nevertheless, approved of his membership on the court as an "impartial, unprejudiced judge."

The trial began in the packed courtroom at the loud command of an impressed, battle-scarred sergeant to "Stand up!"

The generals filed in to take their places, the tinkling and jingling of their medals being the only sound to reach the ears of the silent, awed audience which had risen quickly to its feet.

Douglas MacArthur was tinkling and jingling with the rest of them in this drama of vindication and retribution. One may be pardoned for wondering now whether this scene ever flashed through MacArthur's mind seventeen years later when he wiped the slate clean at Bataan, his grimy men fighting like tigers in the "foxholes," after the Japanese had destroyed the pitiful air force, he had in the Philippines.

For a time, the trial seemed to be turning in Mitchell's favor. With the nation watching every move it made, the prosecution found it impossible to prevent the flyer's charges from being aired.

Congressman Reid had shrewdly pounced upon an address President Coolidge had delivered the previous June before the graduating class at Annapolis advocating free speech for naval officers:

"The officers of the Navy (said the President) are given the fullest latitude in expressing their views before their fellow-citizens, subject, of course, to the requirements of not betraying those confidential affairs which would be detrimental to the service. It seems to be perfectly proper for anyone upon any suitable occasion to advocate the maintenance of a Navy in keeping with the greatness and dignity of our country. But as one who is responsible not only for our national defense, but likewise our friendly relations with other people, and our title to the good opinion of the world, I feel that the occasion will very seldom arise and I know it does not now exist, when those connected with our Navy are justified, either directly or by inference, in asserting that other specified powers are arming against us...."

"All that Colonel Mitchell did," Congressman Reid said, "was to seek to tell the people of a situation and bring about an adequate and well-balanced national defense, as President Coolidge has urged. Yet there are some who seem small enough to condemn him for a patriotic act. It is the duty of all to do as Mitchell is doing, that is, to get before the country the facts in a matter vital to the national defense."

Was Mitchell to be denied the right of criticisms which were mild in comparison with the denunciatory language of General Hooker, General McClellan, Colonel Theodore Roosevelt and Admiral Sims? Could there be a greater contrast than was afforded by the wisdom of such Presidents as Lincoln, McKinley and Theodore Roosevelt and the action of the martinets in time of peace who would punish faithful officers for timely and vigorous warnings?

Brave words by Mitchell's counsel, but too much for at least one of the glowering generals of the court, who muttered: "Damned rot!" The expression was shouted out later by the same general over Reid's emphatic protest when Mitchell's evidence was finally forced into the record. Those who described Billy Mitchell as pale and nervous when he took the stand to defend himself did not know that the great strain of his activities had already begun to undermine him. In the stress of excitement his heart, as he told his intimates, "pounded the breath" out of him.

But he was soon composed. He recited the story of his career simply, his voice rising to denounce the DH's which had killed his men in France, and which were still killing them on our training fields.

The "flaming coffins," he called them. "It constitutes criminal negligence to keep using flying ships of that kind!"

He was asked regarding the charge he had made that air officers were "bluffed and bulldozed" so that they did not dare to tell the truth to Congressional Committees.

"I was bluffed and bulldozed, for one," he replied.

"Did you tell the truth?"

"Yes, but other officers were afraid to tell the truth."

Almost with amusement Billy Mitchell reviewed his experiences in bombing the German battleships off Cape Hatteras. He had been ordered by nervous "battleship admirals" to operate at 10,000 feet, "when as a matter of fact we had no bombers able to make the height."

It was a deliberate effort, he said, to hamper the chances of the airmen. "Damned rot," muttered the general again. Repeated assaults by Major Gullion apparently had little effect upon the accused beyond stirring him at times to heated, if not angry denunciation of the War and Navy systems for control of aviation. He charged that high Army and Navy officers had given Congress misleading information, and that the Navy's one airplane carrier, the Langley, "was worthless and obsolete."

There was much he wanted to tell for the court record, warnings he had sounded to the nation, but the generals refused to hear him.

He was being tried for insubordination. This was not an assembly to seek his advice on national defense.

He managed in one outcry to assert himself and bring the crowd almost out its chairs while the head of the court, flushing with anger, commanded silence.

"Four thousand fighting planes can be built for the cost of a great battleship!"

"Stop this preposterous propaganda!" shouted Major General Howze, the president of the court.

"He's still trying to slide-in his insidious and nationally disturbing hallucinations," Major Gullion added, shaking his finger at the accused.

The court would not listen to a truth which, seventeen years later, was to be accepted reluctantly as an inexorable fact. Battleships could be sunk by airplanes. A battleship cost between $50,000,000 and $70,000,000. But that was just the beginning of the waste. It then required, for its protection, one cruiser costing between $20,000,000 and $30,000,000; four destroyers costing $3,000,000 to $4,000,000 each; four submarines, a personnel of a thousand men and dockyards and supply facilities—a total of $100,000,000. And a battleship must be replaced after a certain number of years so that it would not become obsolete.

Some of these facts Billy Mitchell managed to bring out until he was muzzled by the court. The generals were more interested in his outburst at the high command. They wanted to know what he meant when he used the language "incompetence," "criminal neglect" and "almost treasonable."

What was "treason," Major Gullion thundered as the generals nodded approval to the prosecutor's new line of attack. Billy Mitchell stood up straight to reply, his service ribbons glowing on his chest, his chin out, his eyes up, while a gathering storm shook the grimy windows in their frames.

"Treason?" he said. "There are two definitions of treason. One is in the Constitution defining treason as aiding the enemy and levying war against the United States. I believe, and I say this without any fear of what you may do to me about it, that the system of the Department of War and the Department of Navy is almost treasonable in that it does not give a proper place to the Air Service of this country in the organization of the national defense of this country!"

Of the seventy or more witnesses who clamored to defend the air crusader were some of America's most brilliant flyers. Captain "Eddie" Rickenbacker, the "Ace of Aces" of the first World War, who had brought down twenty-six German planes, the highest number destroyed by any American, upheld all of Mitchell's contentions in impassioned testimony. When asked by Major Gullion if he were acquainted with the war equipment of the Army Air Service which was still in use, Rickenbacker replied wryly, that he was.

"What should be done with it?" queried Gullion, extending his arms out helplessly.

Rickenbacker snapped back: "The graveyards of the country show that we ought to get rid of all of it!"

Supporting Mitchell again, Rickenbacker said it was "suicide" to fly without parachutes, that parachutes were as necessary to a plane as life preservers were on board a ship. Mitchell had made a similar claim when he charged the Navy with "criminal negligence" for not providing parachutes on the Shenandoah. The famous ace thundered against the folly of relying upon anti-aircraft fire to repel an air attack. "Such battles will have to be won in the air."

He had flown 300 hours over enemy territory, and enemy anti-aircraft fire had never prevented him from carrying out his mission.

"Remember," he said with great intensity, as he closed his testimony, "the United States, which invented the airplane, ranks eight right now in air power. The countries ahead of her, in the following order, are France, England, Italy, Germany, Russia, Japan and Poland."

There were other great airmen to flock to Mitchell's defense: Lieutenant Leigh Wade of America's Round-the-World flight, Reed M. Chambers, "runner up" to Rickenbacker; Harold L. George, who was to become a brigadier in the Second World War to direct the Ferrying Command; Lewis Hyde Brereton, to be a major general in 1942 in charge of American Air Forces in India and China. These were all air enthusiasts of the first rank, zealous admirers of the air genius.

One man among them was to go farther than the rest; Major Henry Harley Arnold, one of Mitchell's boys – "Happy" Arnold, whose warnings were taken by the court-martial to be merely the wanderings of a mind disordered by Mitchell's hypnotic spell.

In 1925, "Happy" Arnold was convinced that battleships were done for, and he said so. He was to see his beliefs verified in 1942 when, white-haired and still grinning, he was to marshal the greatest air force in the world with six continents as his battlefield. Such were the men whose conclusions were thrown into the wastebasket by the military gentlemen who were trying Billy Mitchell.

While Arnold was testifying for his former Chief, Brigadier General Fechet flew over the capitol for maneuvers, and perhaps to reassure Congress.

"There goes all our air force," Major Arnold asserted, pointing upward. "It has thirty-five planes, the largest number we could muster to defend Washington!"

Even Congressman LaGuardia, later to become the little mayor of the big city, took the stand to warn the nation that New York was not properly protected against air attacks. The National Guard of his state, he said, was given obsolete planes by the Army. He ridiculed the anti-aircraft tests at Fort Tilden, and readily admitted before the incensed generals that he had told the newspapers, "Billy Mitchell was being tried by nine dog-robbers of the General Staff."

As testimony progressed it was disclosed that President Coolidge was Mitchell's chief accuser. Secretary Davis, who never admitted that he was carrying out the President's orders, was named in the same category. The press of the nation was devoting its main space to the trial. To the thinking public, Mitchell's charges, corroborated by such witnesses, had become matters of grave consideration. They involved for instance, the lamentable defenses of Hawaii, based on reports of his own investigations; the fact that by procrastinating, the administration had let slip through its fingers the Central American commercial lines, which would eventually place the Panama Canal in danger.

The assertion, referring to the Canal, by Major Raycroft Walsh had disturbed the General Staff profoundly. The German dirigible expert, Captain Anton Heinen, had vociferously supported Mitchell with the testimony that the reduction of safety valves had caused the wreck of the Shenandoah.

And so, it went, in at one ear and out of the other of the obstinate men hearing the evidence. "Rome endured as long as there were Romans," shouted Congressman Reid, the flyer's counsel; "America will endure as long as there are Mitchells!"

Brigadier General Fechet, who had fallen into Mitchell's job as Assistant Chief of the Air Service could not let his old buddy down. He rose to his defense during the trial, at a banquet at the Hotel Astor in New York: "Some will say there is no doubt that Colonel Mitchell was insubordinate, but I know that he felt it was the only way to put his views before the country. I am not the one to say he was not right!"

For seven weeks, Mitchell was to be held in the public pillory of this trial, destined to be one of the most historic in the records of armies. Fearful of public reaction, the War Department (having received barrels of letters from irate and badly-informed citizens who wrote that under no circumstances would the nation permit Billy

Mitchell to be shot), issued a public announcement that the most serious consequences he could suffer under the circumstances was to be dismissed from the Army.

"No sentence," stated the War Department publicly, "may be imposed which would hold him up to public ridicule and scorn. Should Colonel Mitchell be convicted the heaviest sentence the Court could impose would be dismissal. Under provisions of the articles cited, he is not liable to any sentence of imprisonment."

The whole tragedy had been summed up by Senator Couzens who urged a unified defense force: "Colonel Mitchell has been actuated by the purest motives of love of country. He deliberately chose a distasteful method of attacking the bitter fruits of bureaucracy, simply because he felt that in no other way could he focus attention upon a desperately important problem. He probably expected discipline."

During Cabinet meetings meanwhile Coolidge tried to mask his nervousness. He was almost alarmed by the news he had read in the newspapers that at the annual dinner of the Aviators' Post of the American Legion on Armistice night, the name of his Secretary of War had been hissed and cat-called and that great cheers had swept the banquet hall when a toast had been proposed to "our savior Billy Mitchell."

He telephoned Davis and the Chief of the General Staff to find out what could be done to "put an end to this circus."

There were more developments to add to the President's disturbance. The powerful Senator William E. Borah, studying matters closely, had come out of his shell to announce that he was "inclined to think Colonel Mitchell correct in his attitude for the consolidation of all our national aviation preparations."

Billy Mitchell, by throwing his career into the balance, had succeeded in bringing the country's most vital defense issue to the man on the street; to be understood by the average American who has to pay the bills. If the meetings of veterans and civilians held all over the nation were an indication of national public opinion, the country was convinced that the crusader was right, and instead of being punished, should be put in charge of America's Air Force and build it up. At the height of the public clamor, Congressman Reid, who had fought as hard and as tirelessly as any man could struggle, almost tooth and claw, for the sake of truth, shook his head. His face revealed his character: dark, frank eyes, a large patient mouth, square jaw and strong cleft chin. He almost equaled Mitchell in energy, which is saying much.

"This is a game with marked cards, Billy," he said (as Mitchell quoted him later), "but we'll go down fighting."

Mitchell was prepared for the verdict of the court. What he was most concerned about was the verdict of the Nation. Was it receiving his message? He knew that past performances meant nothing in the battle he was engaged in. If you lost, obscurity was the penalty. It was a kind of concomitant to greatness, as satires and invectives were an essential part of a Roman triumph, as he had read somewhere. The men he fought were using a language unintelligible to him. Their abstract terms were shadows that hid a vacuum.

They expected him to carry a lantern without a light. "I've found out one thing," he remarked at that time with a grin. "Martyrdom in our advanced state of civilization is not on the decline."

"I'll shoulder my pack," he said, "but I will not pass into the desert."

He was never to forget the impressions the trial was to make upon him. The real story of it, he believed, had never been completely told. Ten years later, when he knew his harassed heart would soon stop complaining, he was toying with an idea for a book.

Half seriously, he said one night at the "Little Venice," that he was almost tempted to call it "The Great American Fool." It would begin with the trial as he remembered it, and include his opinions of the men clashing in an arena which his crusade had created. "I could almost predict the future of some of them," he said. "They will regret what they did. I wouldn't want anything in this world but ten years more of life. Everything will be settled during that time for a thousand years."

In this mood Billy Mitchell prepared a batch of copy, much of which he wrote himself, the balance being dictated to one of the authors of this work.

"I'll give it to you," he said, "to do with it what you wish. One of these days it'll become news. Right now, the publishers tell me they're fed up with airplanes."

His conclusions, interesting because of his vaulting mind, his estimates of men, such as Douglas MacArthur, for instance; his inclination to search the future, are printed in the two succeeding chapters because of a promise given to him on his deathbed.

10 - THE NINE MORROW MEN

The following chapter, composed of material left with Emile Gauvreau by General Mitchell, less than three months before his death, may have been projected by the air crusader as part of a frank autobiography which he hoped to be able to write; perhaps to be published posthumously, because of its implications. The General felt at the time, and told intimate friends, that he was losing a battle with a heart ailment, from which he died on February 19, 1936. Although much of his manuscript may not be printed now, such parts of it as can be used are of singular interest because of their note of ominous warning of the present war, of the inevitability of which the General was convinced, through his sources of private information. His conclusions concerning some of the national figures who opposed his ideas and beliefs are here for the first time made public.

I THINK IT IS SAFE TO ASSUME THAT I shall not be charged with emotional judgment when this appears in print because everything I have said about airplanes and battleships will be verified in the war in which we will be involved, and which will be upon us in less than five years. I feel I will not be with you then. I say that as a soldier who has faced death and who knows what it is. One who has inherited a tradition, an instinct, almost, for the military, from his family, can speak of this.

My own conclusions about the men who tried me, who were not looking for the truth and who will pass under this review had better be left for the printed page after I have disappeared from the scene of controversy between aircraft and sea craft. Some of these men perhaps tried to be sincere. They had been among my best friends, but they were afraid of a truth which will revolutionize warfare for the next thousand years. It was too much for some people to believe. A number of the men who convicted me will be called upon again to guide this nation in the second World War, in all probability. I hope they will then understand what I had to say. Douglas MacArthur, I believe, will be the first to admit that I was right, when the next war comes. He regrets the part he played in my court-martial. May he be brave enough to say so openly. He will go far if he can extricate himself from the stupidities of our War Department and if he is given free rein in whatever he may be doing. I hope he will not discover the truth at the cost of his life. As a General, I know men. He is that kind of man.

I welcomed my court-martial because it was the only opportunity afforded to me to bring to light officially all of my views on the misuse of the airplane for military purposes. I wanted an airing of my criticisms. I wanted the people to hear and decide. Those on the board were powerful enough to see to it, however, that my purpose was only partly accomplished. I had no doubt of the result when I walked in to be tried. I did not go into this fight to save my military career, as the newspapers said. I wanted to save the country by making it hear the truth. The court announced, as the trial began, that 'the issue is not the truth or falsity of what Mitchell said, but whether or not what was said tended to disrupt discipline.' The Army, someday, I hope will outgrow such stupidities.

There were some fearless men, astute enough to anticipate what would happen to me. My good friend LaGuardia, then a Congressman, was the first to say that I was not being tried by a jury of my peers but by officers who were prepared to find me guilty. That was the truth of it. But on the witness stand in my defense and under cross-examination he softened his statement, for diplomatic reasons, I suppose, by saying that when he had made it, he did not know that Douglas MacArthur was on the court. Even now, LaGuardia says funny things.

Looking back, I see almost an ironical touch of fate in the disagreement between these two men about my contentions. Perhaps by now MacArthur knows that the fog of the next war will not be confined to the battlefield. LaGuardia knew it long ago from experience and if he should be a war mayor of New York he will shoulder a responsibility as heavy as ever rested on a general's shoulders. He will know what to do to prepare his city for a bombing which even now is entirely feasible.

He knows the danger as I do. As far back as 1925 he said: 'There would be no trouble at all to attack New York from the air if the protection was only an anti-aircraft defense.' Let those words remain in the minds of the people. I know from my own knowledge that Germany, during the last war, had airships prepared to bombard New York. This testimony was greeted with laughter before a House committee after I had returned from France.

As my remarks prompted by the disaster of the dirigible Shenandoah led to my court-martial, I can look back with a feeling of pity upon Rear Admiral William A. Moffett whom I survive. He was chief of the Naval Bureau of Aeronautics when he charged me with falseness and vindictiveness. I had opposed his methods of operation for years. He knew little about lighter-than-air craft and was directly responsible for the catastrophes we suffered then and subsequently in that branch of the service. Perhaps he was my bitterest enemy because of my criticisms of his ignorance. But he was brave in death. His words, during my trial, nevertheless reflected the thick-headedness and rancor of the General Staff and the Navy.

The most charitable way to regard these (Mitchell's) charges is that their author is of unsound mind and is suffering from delusions of grandeur... The revolutionary methods of the Communists have been invoked to overcome the opposition of loyal men who have sought to thwart the ambition of unscrupulous self-seekers... Instead of an eagle soaring aloft with eyes for the country's defense, we have, instead, one who really played the part of a vulture swooping on its prey once it is down!

The only answer that I could make to Moffett's remarks was that he would inevitably be ruined because of his lack of knowledge of lighter-than-air mechanism, which was beyond his imagination to control. Eight years later, when he went down with seventy-three of his men in thirty seconds in the Akron, off Barnegat Lightship, in the fury of a storm he insisted upon meeting head-on, the tragedy may have been too sudden for him to recall my warning. So much for the obstinacy of brave men!

Perhaps my court-martial might have taken a different turn but for an official report presented to President Coolidge on December 2, 1925, while I was being tried, and sixteen days before I was found guilty. Ironically enough, the report was made by the President's Air Board, appointed at my suggestion in September of that year, consisting of nine members headed by Dwight W. Morrow as chairman, then a lawyer and a banker and a member of the firm of J. P. Morgan & Co. I had a high regard for his ability as an organizer during the last war which brought him the award of the Distinguished Service Medal from General Pershing for 'exceptionally meritorious and distinguished services' in connection with shipping of war materials as a member of the Military Board of Allied Supply. I learned, to my regret, after his appointment that he did not believe the airplane would ever play a major part in any war in which we might be involved.

It impressed him, however, as the basis of a great money-making industry which should be encouraged to sell without limit our best aircraft to foreign powers, then already bidding for our modern equipment, notably Japan. Morrow believed that we were safely protected between two oceans and that any theory involving air offense on our part bordered on the ridiculous.

IN THESE CONCLUSIONS HE WAS warmly supported by President Coolidge, who, until his death, accepted the airplane as an interesting invention which had proved of little purpose in the last war, but which undoubtedly might be developed to carry passengers who were in a foolish hurry, but who might reach their destination with more safety than speed by riding on trains. Whether Morrow changed his attitude two years later when his future son-in-law, Charles A. Lindbergh, flew the Atlantic, is a matter which the banker rarely discussed—in public, at least.

As events transpired, had Morrow lived, Lindbergh's reputation would have been used to assist Morrow in obtaining the nomination for the Presidency. The Morrow Air Board, however, before Lindbergh streaked the skies, was stuffed by financiers (of the aircraft industry) and their findings were to result in practically our whole aviation development being turned over to a gigantic money-making monopoly. The report which Coolidge adopted eliminated not only the pioneers in aviation but the very highly trained government personnel which we had developed during arid just after the war. The Board made no attempt to support any definite concrete policy except to make money. I have expressed this conclusion many times.

I had been hopeful of the Board's investigation, as I had been informed, after I had suggested its appointment, that it would make a thorough study of my recommendations for a separate service under a Secretary of Air to direct all activities of the Bureau of Aeronautics.

This had been my idea for many years. It is still a good one. President Coolidge had announced that the Commission had been selected 'for the purpose of making a study of the best means of developing and applying aircraft in national defense (without regard for any activities of offense which might be necessary in the future) and to supplement the studies already made by the War and Navy Departments.'

Even at this date (December 5, 1935), with our potential enemies already armed to the teeth for a devastating war of the air, the report still holds for the thinking public a ghastly significance. Coolidge read it in peace and comfort, and made notes from its information for a message to Congress, as I recall. The Morrow Board's findings retarded our progress in aviation for ten years and will be responsible for whatever disasters we may experience if we are plunged into war without an adequate air arm to save us. By the time Coolidge received the report the court-martial had discredited me in the eyes of those in power to such an extent that I did not expect any of my recommendations to be adopted.

The newspapers referred to the fact that the Morrow Board had thrown out what they referred to as my 'pet scheme' for a unified air service. The commission had to admit that the country lacked a consistent and continuing national air policy, a conclusion which might have been reached by an intelligent lieutenant at any one of our retarded airfields. Its chief recommendation consisted of twin five-year development programs for the Army and the Navy.

We do not consider, the Commission reported, that air power as an arm of national defense has yet demonstrated its value, certainly not in a country situated as ours, for independent operations of such a character as to justify the organization of a separate department. We believe that such independent missions as it is capable of can be better carried out under the high command of the Army and the Navy, as the case may be.

I hope these conclusions may never have to be reversed in the middle of the coming War of the Air when our security as a Nation, if I am any judge, will be hanging in the balance. When war comes, remember the following words of the report from the nine misguided Morrow men:

"There is no danger of direct air attack from foreign countries. There is no airplane at the present time capable of making a trans-ocean flight carrying a useful load of bombs... It further appears that in order to place any considerable enemy air force in position for effective operation against our cities, ground armies or military positions, it would be necessary to transport such force by water-borne shipping—airplane carriers and cargo ships—and establish a land base from which such operations could be carried on. This could not be effected so long as our fleet is undefeated on the sea."

All this, in the face of the fact that by 1919, six years previously, the principal factors that govern and dominate military aviation had been discovered. To open-minded scientists even in 1903 when Orville Wright conquered the air with what appears on the records as the world's first sustained airplane flight, the Morrow report would have been received as a first-class example of arrested development.

What had been going on in the air from the time the war ended until 1925 had been cast aside by the Morrow Board. They saw no significance in Harry Hawker's almost successful flight from Newfoundland to the British Isles in 1919.

The same indifference was displayed to the accomplishment of Lieutenant Commander A. C. Read, during the same year when he flew, with stops along the route, from America to England in a seaplane. The committee had forgotten the famous flight of Captain John Alcock and Lieutenant A. Whitten Brown in 1919, when they flew a Vickers Vimy from Newfoundland to Ireland, a distance of 1,890 miles by a direct hop in fifteen hours, fifty-seven minutes. All this was before Lindbergh's hop.

No impression had been made on the Morrow Board by the flight in 1919 of the British Airship R34 which crossed from the British Isles to the United States and back again. In that year Captain Ross Smith and his brother, Lieutenant Keith Smith in a Vickers Vimy had proved that air connection between Great Britain and Australia was an accomplished fact.

In 1920 came the historic flights from England to Cape Town, South Africa. In 1919 the Dutch Airline had already been founded, to reach out to the most distant Dutch colonies with Fokker airplanes of remarkable reputation for reliability.

By 1924 Amsterdam was already in touch with Batavia by air. Even while the Morrow Board's report was being written in November 1925, Sir Alan Cobham was making his space-eliminating flight from England to Cape Town, to return home in the same machine.

These great developments in the air meant nothing to the Morrow men who clung to the idea that any attack upon the United States from the sky would have to be made by airplanes transported by waterborne shipping! Christ save us in years to come from such mentality in high places!

Perhaps the most damnable recommendation of the report, which, when war comes, will inevitably result in the destruction of our own men by airplanes sold to Germany, Japan and Italy by American manufacturers is contained in the following paragraph printed in letters of infamy in the government records of the Coolidge Administration:

The board urges the encouragement of civilian aircraft and the sale of planes to foreign countries so as to lessen the number of planes which the government must order to keep the industry in a strong position.

It appears impracticable,' the Board continued, 'to make definite plans for the size of the air force at some period ten years or more distant, and for the amount and type of equipment to be bought each year to reach a goal. Conditions change too rapidly. To select a given type of machine would choke inventions.

Death in a dunce's cap must have grinned when the board held up for praise the murderous DH machine, the 'flaming coffin' of the last war, which killed more 'of our flyers than the Germans did. Our pilots still were compelled to fly these crates eight years after the Armistice. Said the Board: "There is no evidence (of the DH's) tending to show basically faulty aerodynamic design, or lack of structural strength as dependent upon design or construction." As the magazine Aviation commented sardonically at that time: "No mention is made of the faithful Jennie which certainly deserves its share of praise, if service counts!"

The Board sounded a note of lamentation regarding the conflicting nature of the testimony it had absorbed, not only in matters of opinion but of actual fact. It informed the President it found it difficult to draw conclusions. 'We are told from one quarter,' the report explained, 'that the United States Army has available for use 1,396 good airplanes, and from another that it has available for use only thirty-four fit to defend us (the latter claim probably being closer to the truth); that America stands far behind Japan in number of airplanes, and that, on the other hand, Japan stands far behind America in available fighting craft; that anti-aircraft fire has no effect upon air attack; that anti-aircraft fire is one of the greatest menaces of air attack.'

But the board was not sufficiently interested to probe any further. The predominating testimony taken down was from manufacturing interests eager to sell to foreign powers, to launch new stock issues and declare dividends. The flyers interviewed by the board were carefully chosen and heads of government departments who were asked for their views were listed beforehand by the Morrow Committee as 'safe men.'

Those who would have been most informative, whose experience was of international scope, who could see ahead fifteen years in the already startling development of aviation and who were clamoring to establish the United States as the leading nation in the air were mysteriously avoided, or treated with indifference if they were interrogated.

Anyone, for instance, who was ready to give his conclusions on a basis of knowledge or experience and who favored a unified Air Force under one directing head, was discredited from the start because of his opinion. All this was not the fault of the people who, trusting as usual, were being led 'back to normalcy' by Big Business.

In discussing the question as to whether aviation should be given a status equal to that of the Army and the Navy the board heard from General Pershing, General Summerall, General Hines, General Ely, Admiral Sims, Admiral Eberle, Admiral Robison, Admiral Coontz and Admiral Hughes and all were opposed to a separate air force. The Board readily concurred with this conclusion, having made its decision even before it had begun to take testimony on the subject, I am convinced. As to naval aviation itself, Morrow's blind men illuminated their findings with the following brilliant conclusions:

We believe the solution [for naval aviation] lies in a broad and generous recognition of Admiral Alfred Thayer Mahan's maxim that a naval officer should have a general knowledge of all branches of his profession and a specialized knowledge of one.

"There is an ignorance almost criminal in this conclusion. It accounted for the fact that the Navy insisted on transferring men from warships to dirigibles and back again for the simple-minded reason that the dirigibles had been put in charge of the Navy. Men were assigned from boats to lighter-than-air craft with nothing but sea-going experience, and tried to buck the storms in the air over the ocean after the manner of a ship holding to its course through gigantic waves. The appalling disasters which followed were not surprising.

One man on the Morrow Committee told me a year later that he had prepared himself for his work by reading Mahan's The Influence of Sea Power upon History, 1660-1783. He might have been better off had he confined himself to Moby Dick.

In years to come, the Morrow report will be studied by students of aviation history as among the blackest pages ever written into our government records. It was laying the foundation for disaster, and whatever losses we may suffer in the coming war can be traced directly to its stultifying and retarding conclusions. I can imagine in years to come the grim laughter which the following paragraph will evoke:

The board found it extremely difficult to get reliable data as to the capacity for building airplanes in the United States. It is estimated that the aircraft industry in the United States can be counted upon to contribute to the air strength of this country during the first twelve months of a major emergency calling for the mobilization of the entire industrial resources and manpower of the nation, approximately 5,000 airplanes.

But a few years later our Air Trust was furnishing more than that number of airplanes to foreign powers alone. The committee avoided with dread the facts of my own predicament as commander of the American Air Force in France when all I could get for my men was 196 machines out of an appropriation of $1,650,000,000. That was the plundering I had come back to fight after the Armistice. War was easier.

But let me drive the facts home, because there are now among us, on the precipice of war, the willful and the greedy in power who never look up, who would build a fence around us and who will tell you that airplanes will never be able to come over here to attack us. They still cling to the criminal folly of the following words which Morrow dictated himself in his committee's findings:

To create a defense system upon a hypothetical air attack from Canada, Mexico or any other of our near neighbors would be wholly unreasonable.

That was as far as they could see! The board looked upon our Air Service as a branch of the Army, an appendage, with a general status which might be similar to the auxiliary role of the cavalry or the infantry and to be supervised by the Secretary of War. It found that the number of our Air Service officers was 912 on June 30, 1925, as against a strength authorized by Congress of 1,247. The committee complacently concluded that our strength of air arm in proportion to the general military establishment compared favorably with that of any other power. This conclusion was completely false and as dangerous as the following philosophy which for years we inhaled as an opiate:

Geographical position with reference to other nations is bound to affect necessary air strength as it affects the rest of the Army.

Among the stupidities of the findings was the statement that, "competition of the Naval Aircraft Factory at Philadelphia has been bad for the industry." Naturally, the manufacturing monopoly, operating under a patent-pool was on the alert to prevent any experiments which it would not be in a position to control. Our government was already in its clutches, and had to take what it could get while our best inventions were sold to our potential enemies.

All this, the board endorsed as good business! One of its definite recommendations brought about the establishment of a Bureau of Air Commerce of the Commerce Department. Under this system the United States suffered more airplane disasters than any nation in the world. One of the Bureau's subsequent directors, Eugene L. Vidal, harassed in his work, even shadowed by private detectives, will, I hope, tell his own story of his experience, someday, for the good of the people.

But so much for the report of the Morrow Air Board whose effect was to have incalculable consequences upon the nation in corroding our thinking as citizens for years to come about the possibilities of Air arm, without which we will be a lost nation. The findings closed with the statement that the committee was animated by a 'spirit of mutual accommodation and understanding' and presented its conclusions with the unanimous backing of all members.

11 - MacArthur Turns His Face

A continuation of General Mitchell's own account of his trial and conviction.

IT WAS MY PURPOSE DURING MY court-martial to let the nation know what I had discovered during my four-year tour of inspection of our air defenses as Assistant Chief of the Air Corps. In this capacity I had been as far away from my country as the Philippines and Hawaii. I had revealed my findings to my counsel, Rep. Reid, an able lawyer whom I respected even though he had told the press, when taking up my case, that I was an 'extremist.'

His righteous wrath was less contained than mine when he was in possession of my findings. These facts, which I had submitted to my superiors, were thrown aside. I don't think they were even pigeon-holed. Most of them were flung into the wastebasket before I was demoted and reduced to a post in San Antonio without any command, much after the manner of a well-meaning cop shunted off his Main Street beat to the sticks by offended politicians.

I remember a gasp from the court-martial board when Reid, referring to the report of my tour of Pearl Harbor and our Hawaiian defenses, announced:

We propose to prove that when Mitchell inspected the Hawaiian services, he found not one single airplane equipped with armament, bomb racks, bomb sights or any accessories necessary to the effective operation of pursuit bombing or observation planes. In the case of the Philippines we will prove an even worse condition. It will be proved that the War Department has been guilty of almost treasonable administration.

As I write this a decade later, during the year 1935 which will soon have ebbed out, my latest information from Hawaii indicates that the condition of our Air Force stationed at that post has not improved to the extent that would be expected in ten years' time. We are vulnerable there because of a criminal disregard of coordination. Our Air Service in Hawaii has been for years nothing, but a football kicked about between the Army and the Navy with an utter lack of cooperation between the military and naval commands in charge.

I presented these discoveries to the War Department long ago but even to this date the reports I receive from my friends are more than disquieting. Good Christ, if people only knew! The bickerings of insect authority, the conflicting orders from Washington, the jealousies, the late hours of social life, the white uniforms in the moonlight, the gold braid, the romantic women, the caressing climate are all part of an existence to lull our men into threadbare security.

I know the human equation and I know the officer's temptations. The true picture of Hawaii, now full of crawling spies, does not add any reassurance to well-informed Americans who are acquainted with Japanese cunning and treachery. Military Hawaii lives under a tradition handed down from one commanding officer to another, to be discussed years later, with a soothing nostalgia, when one returns home to the soft chairs of the Army and Navy clubs, the head resting back, the eyes closed, the jowled face smiling, the paunch expanded, the tinkling glass in hand, the toasts to Mahan. Ah, those good old days in Hawaii! Planes? Why, the Navy could clean up those little yellow-bellies before dinner time!

That talk will go on until we have been sent reeling from a blow delivered by our own ignored invention in the hands of our enemies, sold to them by our own betraying manufacturers wearing the decorations of the governments who would destroy us! The airplane is the seeing eye of our outposts.

Reconnaissance from the air is the only means of warning Hawaii and the Philippines of the sneaking approach of our mortal enemy in the Pacific. We should have built underground bases for planes at those strategic points ten years ago.

A Secretary for Air freed of the doddering Winfield Scotts of the War Department would have seen to all this. The fighting plane and the bomber, ever on the alert and in scattered formation when resting on their bases furnish the only hope of defense for Pearl Harbor. If our warships there were to be found bottled up in a surprise attack from the air and our airplanes destroyed on the ground nothing but a miracle would help us to hold our Far East possessions. It would break our backs. The same prediction applies to the Philippines, which would be at the mercy of squadrons of bombers, our warships paralyzed or scuttling for cover.

Japan has known this for ten years, if we don't; and if we have to learn our lesson by such a tragedy our last battleship will have been built in less than a year after the Japanese have sprung at us. Warships will be useless without aircraft to protect them as a sky blanket.

I know, because I have sunk battleships with nothing but a crate to fly me. I have preached this doctrine for seventeen years and it will be driven home in the next war when admirals, I swear, staggering on their punctured decks, stare into the sky white-faced and helpless.

Then, on the doorstep of our stupidity and obstinacy may be placed the responsibility for the unnecessary loss of life to follow until we have been restored to our senses. But until that happens, untold millions of dollars will be wasted for battleships by fools in authority who persist in treating our Air Force as a stepchild. There can be no better example than Hawaii of the desperate need of a separate Air Force under a single command.

It is interesting to note, at this late date, that the report of my discoveries in Hawaii caused a flare-up just as my court-martial was getting underway. Major General Charles P. Summerall, who had been selected as president of the court had been in command in Hawaii when I had made my findings of the conditions under his jurisdiction.

He looked upon the criticism as a personal affront and had written a letter at the time which was in violent disagreement with my conclusions. He had denied what I had seen with my own eyes. He had opposed before the Morrow Board my recommendations for a separate Air Service and without directly identifying me had denounced me in a public address.

I challenged him as a prejudiced member of the court that was to try me and with some reluctance he requested to be excused. His departure, I felt, would not have much bearing on the outcome, anyhow. The court knew from the beginning what the General Staff expected of it.

My Hawaiian discoveries were brushed aside angrily by the men who were trying me. All they cared to establish was whether I had been guilty of breaking their gag-ruled discipline. I was bursting with my information, but I never would have broken through the entrenched forces of the embalmed heads of our Army and Navy had I not shouted it out to the public. When will these martinets ever learn that they are in charge of the people's army?

It was worth the price of conviction to let the nation know the truth, which was being choked at its source. All of it was as true in 1925 as it is now, ten years later. But even before my trial opened the General Staff had been thrown into such alarm by the recognition the news columns had given me that military publicists were appointed to visit editors and urge them to print material inimical to my own interests; which were always the country's interests.

James T. Williams, Jr., editor of the Boston American was a notable witness who bared this chicanery.

I was not surprised to discover that the White House had failed to produce the complete files of the Morrow report which I had hoped to use in my own defense. Vital letters from the White House to the Morrow Board were denied to me. The public probably will never know the details of those findings whose private data Coolidge kept to himself.

What I received of the report was not much more than had been given to the newspapers. Wranglings in court and spasmodic objections blocked nearly every attempt on the part of my counsel to make public the conditions I wanted to reveal.

But at times the prosecution was unable to keep the lid down on its skullduggery. The disaster of the Shenandoah, naturally, could not be ruled aside as irrelevant. My statements about it had directly involved me in the trial. The widow of the dirigible's commander, Mrs. Zachary Landsdowne, appeared shrouded in mourning to swear that an aide to Wilbur, Secretary of the Navy, had sought to influence her testimony through an acquaintance, to whitewash the catastrophe. I still feel that this was done without Wilbur's knowledge, though men as high have stooped lower.

Commander Landsdowne had told his wife before embarking on his flight across the country that the trip was of a dangerous nature and unnecessary. He had been sacrificed with his men on a barnstorming expedition to fly over state fairs to satisfy vote-begging Congressmen.

Slowly, the ghastly affair was unfolded at my trial. At times the purpose of my defense could not be entirely sidetracked. Rear Admiral Sims, then retired, assailed the officers in control of the Navy as ignorant and unfit and predicted that the last battleship had been built. Brigadier General Hugh A. Drum rose to fantastic heights by angrily bellowing that to compel the evacuation of the District of Columbia by air attack, an enemy would have to drop more than 9,573,000 pounds of mustard gas, and that to place the gas, 2,000 bombers would be necessary.

Major General Amos Alfred Fries was more conservative with his estimate of 1,000 bombers and twenty tons of gas. These assertions, of course, were introduced to ridicule my warnings that fleets of planes could destroy a city. Those excited men in that courtroom, who may survive me, are likely to see in their lifetime a corroboration of their own words, even though they were used in exaggeration.

Fighting from my side of the barricades was an officer whose convictions and courage may help to bring our Air Force to its required strength before the next war comes upon us. He was Major H.

H. Arnold, one of my boys, fearless before his bigoted superiors. He attacked bitterly the use of the obsolete planes we had to work with and produced a long list of figures showing the casualties which these machines had caused.

He knew his 'flaming coffins' still on our fields for training purposes with their murderous record of twenty-six fatal accidents and thirty-eight deaths in 1924; thirty fatal accidents and forty-five deaths during the year my trial was underway. Arnold, God bless him, spoke it all out. He produced records of the Air Service to show that 517 officers and men had been killed between 1919 and 1925.

The court, in the face of this indictment of the DH's, twiddled its thumbs. It was to pay no attention to it. I pitied Arnold who had to send his men up, even in peacetime, in the same suicidal crates which had killed my boys in France. My own brother died in the Air Service. Arnold, at the risk of his own position, defied the Morrow report with these words:

> To make matters worse, while we are training in obsolete planes, our service does not compare favorably with the foreign services. That is more than an opinion. Statistics show that we have only eight pursuit squadrons while England already has thirteen; France thirty and Italy twenty-two. My opinion is based on my fourteen years in the Air Service, Gentlemen. We shouldn't be in this condition.

But the court was more interested in a letter written on March 24, 1925 to President Coolidge by Weeks, then Secretary of War, which it produced on the eve of my conviction with the sly approval of the White House and which Major General Dennis E. Nolan, acting Chief of Staff, read to the crowded room with relish and ringing tones. Its words were enough to foretell the outcome of my trial:

> His (Mitchell's) course is so lawless, so indicative of personal desire for publicity at the expense of everyone with whom he is associated that his actions render him unfit for a high administrative position such as he now occupies.

General Nolan reiterated the testimony of General Staff officers that the War Department was opposed to my plan for a unified Air Service. He spoke like a trained parrot. He insisted that the present and 'satisfactory' organization of the 'Air Service branch' was directly attributed to General Pershing himself, a man who had never set foot in a plane. At least, I never met a man who saw him in one.

I could see little use in a prepared argument which my counsel proposed to make in my defense and refused to permit him to present it. The trial had reached its farcical limits. I decided to rise in my own right and sum up the persecution in a nutshell.

I remember MacArthur lowering his eyes and turning his face away. Others on the trial board, who had been my friends, bowed their heads as they sat, not in judgment, but as marionettes manipulated by the strings of the President and the General Staff determined to take me to the block.

My statement may be remembered, when we have at last recognized the airplane as the greatest arm of modern warfare:

"My trial before this court-martial is the culmination of the efforts of the General Staff of the Army and the General Board of the Navy to depreciate the value of air power and keep it in an auxiliary position which absolutely compromises our whole national defense."

The curtain was coming down on the farce. I settled back in my chair like a man composing himself in an air shelter before a bombing raid. Major Allen W. Gullion had been chosen to handle the heaviest batteries in the summing up. Colonel Sherman Moreland was to assist him with a few parting shots, but his face reddened with discomfiture when the crowded courtroom burst into spontaneous laughter upon his declaration that the obsolete DH plane, the 'flaming coffin' of the Army Air Service was 'the Cadillac of the air.' He turned about in anger, pointing at me with a trembling finger: 'Expel from your midst anybody not meeting the requirements of patriotism!'

I remember Gullion licking his dry lips feverishly with a darting tongue and riffling through his notes. I knew what to expect from him, an army careerist, shrewdly climbing his way up, rung by rung, from one post to the next, serving his branch of the service as a smart politician clings to his party. Those above him said he had the 'right background' and praised his adaptability.

He could boast, at the time, of his professorship of Military Science and Tactics at the University of Kentucky which presumably wasted no time on the study of 'fool killers,' as airplanes were called in Professor Gullion's neck of the woods. But he has come up since then: through the General Service School, the Army War College, the Naval War College, on the General Staff Corps Eligible list, and in his back pocket an honorary degree of LL.D., from the University of Hawaii. I wonder if he remembered a word of the conditions I disclosed when he became senior judge advocate of the Hawaiian Department.

Of course, it may be correctly pointed out that flying never came under his jurisdiction after he got through with me. My trial was a good stepping-stone for him, and no man could have been more sure-footed when he came before the court to tell that body exactly what it expected to hear.

"Fail to dismiss this man," he screamed in a high-pitched voice, "and you weaken the authority of every commissioned and non-commissioned officer in the service. Dismiss him as he deserves, and you strengthen the arm of every single officer commanding a company from Marfa to Nogales; dismiss him for the sake of the young officers of the Army Air Service whose ideals he has shadowed and whose loyalty he has corrupted. Dismiss him in the name of truth, under whose aegis he has sought protection, but whose face he does not know. Our soldiers are watching this case in Camp Stotsenburg, in Schofield Barracks, in Tientsin, at Governor's Island. Throw him out! We ask it in the name of the American people whose fears he has played upon, whose hysteria he has fomented, whose confidence he has beguiled and whose faith he has betrayed!"

"Is Mitchell a Moses?" shouted Gullion, the veins standing out on his temples. "Is he a Moses fitted to lead the people out of a wilderness which is his own creation only? Is he the George Washington type as his counsel is trying to make us believe? Is he not rather of the all-too-familiar charlatan and demagogue type, like Alcibiades, like Catiline, and except for a decided difference in poise and mental powers, in Burr's favor, like Aaron Burr?"

I heard from his companions later that Gullion had been rehearsing his speech before a mirror. "Dismiss from us," he continued, his hands held up in horror with the attitude of a Bible ranter, "this flamboyant self-advertiser, this widely imaginative, hobby-riding egomaniac, always destructive, never constructive except in wild, non-feasible schemes and never overly careful as to the ethics of his methods."

There was more of this. One point of Gullion's attack might have impelled me to throttle him but for the fact that I gripped my chair and held my seat. He attempted to show that my book Winged Defense, which had just been recently published was made up of a mass of stolen material. I was proud of that book. Years of experience from the time that Orville Wright had taught me to fly, had gone into it. But it had had a disturbing effect on the General Staff, which was ignoring every one of the warnings I had printed in it. Figuratively, it had to be burned by the Army's witch doctors. "He cribbed it!" shouted Gullion. "He cribbed it, page after page!"

This lying assault was finally stopped by Congressmen Reid who said Gullion would not be permitted to try a copyright case before a court-martial. My counsel was sustained, but Gullion, as though wound up for a filibuster, swerved into new channels of slander. At times his words seemed to pour out of some cavernous mouth of the Dark Ages.

Before Gullion had put down his lash, staggering to his chair, exhausted and choking with his own fury, he had flayed mercilessly, without a grain of fairness, every man who had dared to appear in my defense.

Of LaGuardia he said with a sneer, "Here is the congressional expert type. A man who comes here to talk about flying with fifteen or twenty hours in the air. He is beyond my powers of description. Thank heaven he is sui generis."

It seemed incredible to believe that men with whom I had hunted and fished, with whom I had ridden at foxhunts, the friends with whom I had touched glasses at the Chevy Chase, at the Rock Creek Hunt, companions who had slapped me on the back, the friends of jolly times, were to lock themselves into a room after hearing my character torn to shreds, and come back, without being able to look me in the face, and say: "Guilty!"

MacArthur, whom I admired for his courage, his audacity and sincerity, surely could not be part of this! But there he was, his features as cold as carved stone. I had fought under his father, General Arthur MacArthur, in the Philippine Insurrection. We had even discussed what might be done someday if Japanese Imperialism should embark on a southward course. And here was his son, a brave soldier, appointed to strip me in mid-career, in an argument over a machine which might someday save the Philippine Islands!

He is back there now (in 1935) directing the organization of the national defense of the Commonwealth government which no battleships could protect from an air attack. Planes and nothing but planes can hold those possessions. Perhaps by this time MacArthur can see it all with an open mind. No man in his position could have a greater opportunity. Something can be learned in ten years; even by some generals.

But MacArthur certainly had not grasped the significance of my trial in 1925. I still believe he erred honestly. Men grow in stature by admitting their own mistakes. Douglas has developed that quality. But perhaps I am a better judge of planes than of men. In the midst of all this clawing, I still remember an unforgettable note of tenderness as my trial came to an end.

My wife appeared in court and held our baby daughter for me to kiss. I recall Will Rogers, his eyes wet and blinking with anger, his lips stern, after listening to Gullion's attack.

"The people are with you Billy," he said. "Never forget that! Keep punching and we'll get somewhere. You can rope 'em."

Suddenly I realized it was all over. Reporters were rushing out with the news that I had been found guilty on all counts. I was sentenced to be suspended from rank, command and duty with the forfeiture of all pay and allowances for five years. The court's 'leniency' had been influenced by my military record, someone was saying.

I stepped out of the ramshackle building into the crisp clean air. There was a low muttering in the crowded courtroom and friends followed me out to the street in little groups with reassuring phrases. "It's going to be O.K., Billy;" "You're bound to win;" "You told 'em!"

The holidays were approaching with their decorations and colored lights. Nothing could have been more cheerful and consoling than that trip home.

'Christmas in Virginia can make one forget anything,' my wife said.

But the implications of my trial were overshadowed, in my mind anyhow, by one great event which no one seemed to associate with my predictions. It seemed to be lost in the sweep of the happenings of the times. It had taken place as my court-martial approached its climax.

Lieutenant James H. Doolittle, the champion aquatic aviator of the Army had set his fourth world speed-record for seaplanes at Bay Shore Park by flying four times over a measured course at an average speed of 245.715 miles per hour. I was interested in Jimmy because, for one thing, he knew Alaska. Previously, that year, Jimmy, who was to become one of the most scientific flyers in the world, had won the Schneider Cup Race. With cool and deadly accuracy, he had written in the sky the answer to my conviction!"

12 - MUFTI

NEWSPAPERS TALKED OF PROSPERITY and bulged with it during the Christmas season of 1925. Most people celebrated the end of the quarter-century with the abandon of the sub-debs of the day who thought life began in speakeasies.

The headlines danced the tune of the money-mad, the underworld politicians, the millionaire bootleggers and the tommy-gun racketeers. In New York the airplane, as news, seemed to have been forgotten, but for one item: an imaginative gentleman who owned a seat on the Stock Exchange had celebrated New Year's Eve as host of a cocktail party in a large-cabined Lockheed Vega 3,000 feet over the Woolworth building. The country embraced Old Guard security, which was to have the same effect on its worshippers that a calm sea has on the Dutch mariner who, it is said, in these circumstances, ties up his rudder, gets drunk and goes to sleep.

At the White House, President Coolidge had dusted the "Mitchell affair" from his shoulder. Such disturbances were bound to happen in a free country in which people talked too much. His message to Congress, communicated through a cornucopia of plenty, saw nothing but years of prosperity ahead.

Thousands of words on the subject were draped under an eight-column heading of The New York Times which had to spill the tidings into the page opposite for two additional columns, giving this treatise of passionate economy a ten-column banner, something almost unique in the history of that calm newspaper. Coolidge now got more pleasure out of the Times than out of the Springfield Republican. He pasted the long heading down carefully and mailed it to his New England admirer, editor Clark, of the Hartford Courant with a curt note:

"Quite sensational for the Times."

The aged editor acknowledged the courtesy with a clipping from his own editorial page on the subject, in which he found himself for the first time in complete agreement with a democratic newspaper.

The Times had much to say about cool Calvin's long-headedness and "mature judgment of the work of administration." It complimented him on "the habits of mind which he brings to all public affairs." [Owner of The New York Times] Mr. Och's [Adolph Simon Ochs, 1858-1935] great paper, with fifty-six pages fairly bursting with the fat of the land, found some room, four days after Mitchell's trial, to note editorially that the court-martial had finished its job:

"It is already evident that the proceedings changed few, if any, opinions... General Hines has promised 2,500 airplanes, twenty airships and thirty-eight balloons... The General Staff members are among the most brilliant and capable officers of the Army..."

Other editorials on the fading topic appeared around the country, all more or less in agreement: a disturber, defying rules of necessary discipline, had compelled his superiors to put him in his place. Wise men had judged. Mitchell was soon forgotten in the news columns but for one final front page flurry.

Congressman Sol Bloom, generally to be found on the barricades with men of goodwill, had proposed the convicted Air Chief to Mayor-elect Jimmy Walker for the post of police commissioner of New York City. The well-meaning Mr. Bloom was certain that Congress would enact any legislation necessary to make the appointment possible. Perhaps he saw in the recommendation something singularly appropriate for a high-flying administration.

Reporters assigned to interview the merry Mayor-elect found him at the old Waldorf making a speech before the annual gathering of the New York Southern Society which had reached the stag-at-eve stage of its proceedings.

Jimmy was pledging to spend a long vacation each winter in the South to honor its hospitality.

"I'll be down," he said, "where the Green River... no, not the Green River, that's a Northern Prohibition product... I'll be down every year where the Swannee River flows!"

Pouring himself into his seat amid the usual applause Jimmy turned to the reporters to straighten them out about Mr. Bloom's interest in Billy Mitchell.

"You mean the guy that flies around and wants to bomb New York?" he inquired with mock alarm. "Off the record, boys, Tammany Hall is up in the air often enough without wings. We're not going to move any bombers into police headquarters. We've got too many pineapples [the Mk. 2 fragmentation grenade, which was used by Prohibition mobsters, including Al Capone] exploding around town already."

The proposal, however, seemed to have been given less frivolous consideration in the company of a future President of the United States. The police commissionership, which had been a job important enough for Theodore Roosevelt, was among other choice political gifts which Walker had to offer, and the prizes were discussed in a secret conference before Governor Alfred E. Smith, the

Mayor-elect, and Tammany Leader George W. Olvany, at a luncheon in the home of Franklin D. Roosevelt.

Apparently, all agreed that Billy Mitchell, as a police boss, would be a bit too much for New York's sensitivities. Olvany is said to have shuddered at the suggestion.

Later, in his office, he remarked, while mopping his red face: "Jesus! Sol Bloom ought to have his bean examined."

A man named Warren, a pale-faced politician got the job. He was to be remembered by the oldest inhabitants as by no means the best police commissioner New York ever had. [Commissioner Joseph Aloysius Warren, one in a succession of NY police chiefs hastily appointed during the violent Prohibition era. Overcome with the mental strain of the job, Warren retired early to a Greenwich, Connecticut sanitarium where he died in 1926 at the age of 44.]

For a few days, newspapermen lived in excited anticipation until the news was given out that Billy Mitchell was beyond consideration as director of the New York police. News writers of the whole country were the air crusader's friend. There was always a good story when he was around.

This view was well reflected by "Iron Hat" Bill Crompton, veteran Park Row authority and spokesman of the "regulars" of the press: "Imagine the headlines if the General got the job and started out by bombing our 50,000 speakeasies! That baby is a ball of fire for circulation. He could make even Brisbane cheer."

At "Boxwood," down in Virginia, Billy Mitchell appeared to be less disconsolate than his remaining disciples.

"He certainly can take it," his friends said.

News editors, appealing to him for comments concerning his trial, had to turn to other subjects for headlines. "I'll let you know," he said, "when the time comes to resurrect me." His counsel, Congressman Reid, expressed his contempt openly for the chicanery behind the General's conviction. Reid was convinced Mitchell was the victim of cowardly and servile men determined to crush the truth, at the expense of the country's safety. Now he understood the passion of the air crusader's outcries.

No longer was Mitchell the "extremist" he had once called him. So deeply had Reid been affected by the ordeal that he had gone to his home in Chicago for a rest.

"Billy Mitchell is the John Brown of 1925," he told the press. "They may think they have silenced him, but his ideas will go marching on, and those who crucified him will be the first to put his aviation suggestions into use!"

Reid's accusations, amounting to a charge of hypocrisy against the court-martial board, the General Staff and the President himself, had the effect of prolonging Coolidge's review of the case. Mitchell, still under the supervision of Army orders, sat at home in silence. He was without pay, without his allowances, even, as a Colonel in the Air Corps. Reid again resorted to the press: "I believe the President will not leave him in this state of slavery."

An impartial board would have acquitted Mitchell or dismissed him from the service. But he had been tried by bureaucrats jealous of their outworn prerogatives, fearful lest the new art of aerial warfare detract from their own importance.

By sending their findings to the White House for review they had ingeniously "passed the buck" to Coolidge who had hoped for the General's outright dismissal.

But at any rate they had satisfied the General Staff. Supporters of Mitchell's cause were being trailed to his home by War Department informers. In his study, the ex-Air Chief, still wearing the uniform of a colonel, collected his papers, studied his maps and jotted down daily notes of his studies. His anger rose to the surface but once.

To his friends he expressed his outraged feelings concerning an aviation scandal which had exploded while he was being tried, for exposing the very conditions which had caused it. The Air Trust, whose tentacles reached into the War and Navy departments was directly responsible for it. Industrial aircraft officials had induced the Naval authorities to send seventeen bombers to Baltimore, to be used to attract crowds for a so-called "air race."

The motives behind this picnic were as shameful as those which had prompted the orders given to the commander of the Shenandoah. Air Trust publicity men at the Baltimore "show" escorted the visiting officers and crews of the bombers to a large suite in a hotel where bootleggers had made all arrangements necessary for revelry.

Gentlemen who handled "public relations" for the aircraft monopoly trooped in with a number of laughing maidens who were to prove to be fatally feminine before the celebration was over.

These rites were called "goodwill work" to keep the Army and Navy aviators in good spirits, and influence them to praise the airplanes the government was forced to buy at grafting prices.

Clouds were lowering as the Baltimore party progressed but the naval aviators, stretched out on divans, drinking liquor held out to them by charming women snuggled beside them, were not interested in weather reports.

When a storm broke over the city with the force of a gale there were but a few officers able to remember their responsibilities.

A handful of them, startled and staring, their white uniforms crumpled and stained, dashed from the suite, begging to be hurried to their bombers which had been left at their moorings without protection, with no one to fly them to safety or even to moor them more securely before the lashing wind did its worst.

Had the officers been present the planes could easily have been flown back to the base at Norfolk. The horrified men saw seven seaplanes totally destroyed under their noses and the other ten planes almost irretrievably damaged; one-third of the Navy's air fleet.

It turned out to be good business for the Air Trust, which received more orders. Nothing was ever done about the outrage, officially, aside from an announcement by Secretary Wilbur that the tender Shawmut had been sent to Baltimore "to aid in the salvage work." Later, a naval court of inquiry convened at Hampton Roads to swing the usual whitewash brush.

"Conditions are frightful," Mitchell blazed, after hearing the account of this disaster from an eye witness. "It couldn't have happened under a unified Air Service."

January of 1926 was half over when he received Coolidge's final thrust. The President was determined to prevent him from talking as an active authority and had upheld the five-year suspension of the court-martial. Mitchell's puny money allowances were to be restored as well as one half of his monthly base-pay as a Colonel; a pittance for courage.

Mitchell had shed more than his own blood in confirmation of his faith. Money, power and officialdom had combined to crush him. Everyone was against him but the man on the street. Little was seen of him now outside of his home. He came down to breakfast in his uniform, neat to the last button. His carved features spread into a tired smile only when he played with his children.

"What are those eagles for, Daddy?"

"They're part of a Colonel's uniform, Billy. You'll wear them someday."

"Do you have to wear a uniform all the time, Daddy?"

"I'm going to wear it as long as I can. It's the best uniform in the world. I was only just growing up when I put it on. I'll wear it as long as I can...."

One day he went upstairs abruptly, leaving Billy and Lucy in bewilderment. The door of his study banged—then silence. Mrs.

Mitchell followed him, stopping on the landing to turn to the children who reflected a strange, invading tension.

"Daddy is tired," Mrs. Mitchell said, but Billy Junior had noticed something more, which he could not understand.

He began to cry a little. "Why," he asked, "did he have tears in his eyes? I saw them. Soldiers don't cry. He told me."

Silence in times of suffering is the best. Mitchell admitted it later when he described the effect upon him of the twelve strokes of the grandfather clock, at midnight, ringing out, day by day, his military career, the brassy notes marching through his study as he paced the floor, a smallish man in regimentals being dragged to fame by persecution.

"Perhaps," he said, "it was the habit I couldn't strip off; not the uniform.

The thought came into my head that if I could keep the uniform on for five years, even if I couldn't do anything, wiser men would come into power and listen to me, like the wrong man put in prison, hopefully waiting. But in five years' time, if I didn't say anything, the whole Air Force might be wrecked.

I knew that we had fewer than fifty military planes of the first class, less than a baker's dozen of pursuit ships. We were practically back to 1917 when I had talked to Wilson. We had at the outside 500 more or less obsolescent planes fit for service. The country had to be told that vastly superior designs were available. But who would do it? Who would fight the Air Trust? Those five years might be fatal to the nation. Suppose war broke out!"

Two weeks after Coolidge had upheld the court-martial's suspension, the Colonel had come to a decision. Seated, still in uniform, under the rays of his study lamp at his crowded desk, and before the great clock below had finished its tired twelfth stroke, he had punctuated the last sentence of a brief note to the President... "and under the circumstances I respectfully request that my commission as Colonel, U.S.A., be vacated at your earliest convenience."

Coolidge, brushing all work aside when he received the letter, snapped up the resignation of the most unerring prophet in 500 years of military history. Who was this upstart to tell the President of the United States that the future was not a prolongation of the past? There had been trouble enough about this newfangled instrument that insisted on leaving the ground, where everybody belonged. Hadn't Pershing denied that it had made history, or would ever make any?

The Chief Executive promptly wiped Mitchell off the Army rolls with his own hard-bitten scrawl, and then, putting down his

Northampton souvenir blotter, he looked again with some curiosity at the note from the man he had stripped. Its brevity pleased him. "He reached the point and stopped," he commented to his secretary.

Suddenly he snapped: "Have something to say; say it; stop when you've done. Tryon Edwards. But who reads him?"

The President's curt reply to "Boxwood," without one word of thanks to the father of the American Air Force for his services, was chucked into Mitchell's mailbox before the sun had set.

The General closed his study door tightly before he read it. Later he walked to his bedroom and stood up straight before his mirror, at attention, chin up. Then, slowly, he began to unfasten the insignia of the rank of Colonel from his uniform, first those which were pinned on.

His fingers trembled a bit as he unloosed tenderly from his collar the "U.S.," and then from his lapels the little wings encircling a globe. He slipped off the Sam Browne gear and the belt at his waist.

Out of his blouse, he stripped the eagles from the shoulders, and cut off with a razor blade the proud spread wings which had been for years on his breast. He put the ornaments carefully in a little lacquered box. He draped the shorn garment in his cupboard and pulled out a suit of black clothes just arrived from the tailor's.

Finally, he began to climb into it. He walked around the top landing in the hall recapturing a thought. He stood uncertainly, at the head of the stairs, fiddling with a black necktie. His voice seemed to falter, and he had to clear his throat before he called out in a tone almost strange down the stairwell.

"Betty ... Betty!"

"Yes, dear." His wife was looking up at him, wide-eyed.

"Tell the boys who are coming for dinner ... tell them I'm wearing a tuxedo."

13 - A Citizen in Action

Newspapers were not kept waiting to print the news of Billy Mitchell's "resurrection." Just five hours after he had received Coolidge's letter, he cracked his demitasse on the table, squared his shoulders in the unfamiliar tuxedo and got up from his dinner party.

His guests, a little in surprise, noted something about him that they remembered as part of him before San Antonio—something peppery in his character had come back, which the word "dashing" was most often used to describe.

"Boys," he shouted, "I'm free. Free as a lark in the sky. I'm my own master. Bragg, call up the Associated Press. I've got something to say."

On the following morning the people knew that Plain Citizen Mitchell was still very much in the ring. Everything he had to say had been ticked off on the wires and headlined across the land.

"I shall tour the country as a citizen to carry straight to the people the story of the true conditions of our national defense. I can do this better than by remaining muzzled in the Army. The Army and Navy bureaucracies have purposely misled Congress and the people and have manipulated the laws so that they can control the armed forces even against the action of the President himself. They have coerced, bulldozed and attempted to ruin patriotic officers. They have actually shaken the land and sea forces in their conception of duty! The military bureaucracy is one of the greatest menaces to our free institutions. The bureaucratic party is more powerful than the Democrats and the Republicans, more powerful than the influence of any creed or sect or religion."

He kept his word, touring the country, lecturing without compensation. The press referred to him as "Citizen Mitchell, the wealthy Virginian stock farmer," a description which drew his laughter. He had never been a wealthy man—far from it—and in his fight for his cause, which was for the people, he drew from his own pocket.

If he had expected to be called "Mr. Mitchell," as he talked through the country in civilian dress, he was to be disappointed. Those who knew him during his tortured year of demotion had never addressed him as "Colonel."

As a member of the General Staff he had entered the World War as a major and had come out of it a General.

No man in that struggle had received as many citations for "repeated acts of extraordinary heroism in action," and his full title was to remain with him until his death in the minds of the people.

"Call me anything you want," he said in those days, "but remember I am a citizen in action."

His activities on behalf of an intelligent air program during the remaining decade of his life—he was to die almost ten years to the day from the time of his "resurrection," as he called it—literally would fill a dozen volumes.

His influence on the public mind, on the thoughts of military strategists of the world, was to be more powerful than it had been when he was "muzzled in the Army."

Publications reflecting the opinions of European governments were to discuss his theories and agree with him, particularly those of the Germans. Experts of foreign powers studied his opinions closely. He was often invited to Europe to express his ideas, all of which were aimed at the future. American bureaucracy in power, however, shunned him as a pariah.

There is notable evidence in Coolidge's addresses, before he announced that he "did not choose to run," that Mitchell's blistering denunciation had got under the President's skin. The Chief Executive read the almost continuous headlines about the man he had reduced to a common citizen with irritation and growing concern.

He decided he would have something to say about aviation in his next annual budget to the Congress. According to one of his aides, he sat at his desk late one night in the White House writing out his thoughts about "airplanes" in longhand.

"Eighty-two million dollars," he muttered, "for those things."

As it was expressed when the newspapers carried the President's message:

"If there is any question as to the failure of our government to recognize the importance of aviation in national defense and commerce, the answer can be found in the vast sums which heretofore have been appropriated and the legislation enacted by the Congress. The estimates contained in this budget carry for this purpose alone a total of more than $82,000,000."

Citizen Mitchell grunted when he read the statement. Now he expressed his disgust of Coolidge openly.

"That's a lot of money for him to count," he said. "As a matter of fact, they've appropriated $82,500,000. How did Calvin happen to forget that extra half million? But the national tragedy of it is that he doesn't know this money is being wasted. We've appropriated more than one billion and five hundred millions in less than ten years, of which more than five hundred millions of dollars have been spent since the Armistice, all thrown away to the Air Trust. It is positively criminal."

Like a hawk circling over a chicken yard, Mitchell soon saw a chance to pounce on Coolidge in a manner which impelled the President to curse.

A furor had developed over the deplorable state of Army housing. General Summerall, Chief of Staff of the Army, had made statements about the condition and was called back peremptorily to Washington from a trip to California.

Mitchell, assuming the role of an astute reporter got the facts of the episode and proceeded to pay his respects to Coolidge with front page articles:

"Upon reaching Washington, General Summerall sat in his chair in uniform for three days without being called by the President. He probably never would have been called, if two prominent newspaper editors had not gone to Mr. Coolidge and told him that he either should get rid of Summerall or tell him what it was all about.

"Mr. Coolidge then had General Summerall brought over to the White House, and hemmed and hawed through an interview with him, in which he told him nothing of constructive value. After this Mr. Coolidge put out a statement that something over $30,000,000 had been authorized for Army housing. This statement is entirely misleading. As a matter of fact, only about $7,000,000 has been appropriated for the purpose and the purpose of Mr. Coolidge's statement was to create the impression in the minds of the public that over $30,000,000 was available."

Reporters found the President in an ugly mood when they went to interview him about Mitchell's accusations.

The Chief Executive was chewing the stump of a cigar and obviously controlling his temper.

"Please do not question me about that man," he said. Reporters, who enjoyed the rumpus, which made salty reading, soon tipped off Mitchell to some facts which served for another explosion. Front pages appeared with large headlines of which the following from a New York newspaper was typical: MITCHELL PLACES MILITARY WASTE AT COOLIDGE'S DOOR, AIR CRUSADER SAYS "NAVY DAY" SHOULD BE CALLED "GRAVY DAY" UNDER PRESENT ADMINISTRATION.

This story was received somewhat like a bombshell in the White House. It contained a direct attack upon the President:

Never in our history have we had an executive so oblivious to the broad principles that underlie our form of government, those of direct-ness, truth and regard for the public welfare. Mr. Coolidge alone is responsible for the monstrous inefficiency and waste that is taking place in our military services.

Coolidge charged with waste! A governor of Massachusetts who used to have his shoes re-soled by a special cobbler who knew how to make them last longer! He had held his first office through his tenacious, pinch-penny method of keeping taxes down. Waste! This was the reward of his public parsimony, scrimping and saving for the people! No charge against him, printed in the press, could have been more painful.

But before he finally packed off for the Black Hills, where he was to announce that he had had enough of public life, Mitchell swooped down on him again in defense of Admiral Magruder who had written articles which pointed out glaring defects in the Navy. The Admiral had been informed that he was to be disciplined by the President.

Mitchell's attack appeared in large headlines in Washington and received national circulation:

"Admiral Magruder has been refused an audience by the National Commander-in-Chief of the United States Army and Navy. He has been turned over to the hangman, in the form of the Secretary of the Navy, a civilian administrator and fiscal bureau chief, who is without command or authority except in the name of the President of the United States. Admiral Magruder, an officer of thirty-five years' service, has the right to see the President, his superior officer, and lay his views before him.

"The Admiral's articles were mild and tempered. He did not tell one half of what should be told. The pork-barrel policy of the administration gets the money out of the people for useless Navy Yards and useless battleships. Mr. Coolidge has held over Congress the whip of patronage, so that most of the members do not dare open their mouths.

"Members of the armed forces are scared into submission by threat of immediate expulsion if they tell the truth to Congress where immunity is supposed to surround everyone who is responsible and who testifies. Mr. Coolidge is responsible for these conditions. He has suppressed free speech, free action, and even free thought on the part of our people."

Mitchell found no hope for his cause when Hoover succeeded the New England groundling in the White House. The General thrust his theories on the attention of the public by prepared speeches which he delivered at important banquets. He pictured future wars which, he said, would be fought almost entirely from the air.

He insisted that airplanes and submarines would be the only valuable instruments of warfare in the next conflict. He visualized pilotless airplanes, flying directly to an objective, dropping bombs and returning.

He predicted the use of aerial torpedoes which would be magnetically attracted by the steel of warships and which would wipe out navies. Many who called him a fool were to read of the destruction of the gigantic cruiser Repulse and the brand-new battleship Prince of Wales, fourteen years later, under the exact circumstances which he had foreshadowed.

The aircraft monopoly, whose ramifications hardly left his thoughts, was becoming his chief point of attack. He trained his guns on the Aeronautical Chamber of Commerce which, he asserted, checked aerial progress, while Herbert Hoover, Jr., employed by the Association, held his job during his father's term as President.

Elliott Roosevelt, son of the President who was to follow Hoover, had also a position with the Association but resigned when he learned that it desired to employ him as a lobbyist, as stated publicly by Representative William I. Sirovich, chairman of the Committee on Patents of the House of Representatives.

Then, one morning, after four years of unending battle against the forces opposed to rapid modernization of air defense, Mitchell shook hands in the White House with a man of many ideas, a man devoted to the people, millions of whom were jobless, on the verge of starvation. Franklin D. Roosevelt had come to head a depression-born administration. The General went back to "Boxwood" more hopeful than he had ever been about American aviation.

"Of course," he said, "Roosevelt has got to take care of the starving citizens first, but he possesses the mind of a man who will understand what the airplane means to this country."

Now the General could almost see the end of the monopoly which had retarded aviation development Surely, Roosevelt's great house-cleaning in national affairs would sweep out the system under which billions of dollars had been wasted in a futile air policy.

Mitchell seemed fortified every time he left the White House.

"The President told me," he said one day, "the way to make dreams come true is to wake up. That's the thought we need behind air defense."

But as time went on, nothing much happened about Billy Mitchell's program. Investigations of monopolies were begun; Wall Street shook with terror, but the Air Trust remained unmolested. The bureaucrats at the War and Navy departments continued undisturbed. Still, the General was hopeful. Early one morning he was summoned to the White House.

The government, in its first effort to break loose from the aircraft monopoly had annulled its airmail contracts with private companies. The Army had been ordered to fly the mail and ten Army flyers had been killed. The Senate stormed with charges of "legalized murder" and "manslaughter."

Mitchell had a well-founded answer for the President who wanted his opinion. "At last, we are discovering," he said, "the appalling state of the most important arm of our national defense. I have been warning the people about this for years. Your decision to annul the contracts, Mr. President, has brought to the surface the terrible condition of our Air Service."

Here was something into which the former Air Chief could sink his teeth. He appealed to the public to understand the situation.

"For years," he wrote to Chairman Black of the Senate Air Mail Investigating Committee, "we were assured by former Administrations and by the civilian air contractors that we had the best air equipment in the world, and it is only through the wise move of the President that we have found out what we really have. The skill, courage and chivalry of our splendid Army flyers have been completely nullified by inadequate equipment and the curtailment by the War Department of the number of hours they were permitted to fly.

"This did not give them an opportunity to perfect themselves in flying through storms and bad weather conditions. It is only through continuing the present mail operations that the true facts can be found out and the remedies applied. Our whole aircraft set-up must be reorganized, and particularly our present aircraft industry, which is controlled and held down by holding companies which have little or no knowledge of aviation.

"It is distressing that the lives of our brave pilots have been lost, but think of what would have occurred to the lives of millions of our innocent population who would be mercilessly annihilated in the next conflict if these facts had not been uncovered. Our national defense, possibly our existence, are really at stake."

The airmail tragedies had vindicated Mitchell. The Army planes which, for years, he had condemned, could not fly even paper! What could they have done in a war? The thoughts passing through the President's mind at the time about the problem were not recorded.

What the administration learned, through a series of almost daily tragedies was that the Army Air Service could not fly the mails with planes it had been forced to buy from the aircraft monopoly. War was only seven years away when the government threw up its hands and returned the airmail to private business.

Of interest in this crisis was a flare-up in the House which concerned a telegram written by Colonel Lindbergh to the President, denouncing the government's attempt to annul its domestic airmail contracts with private companies. Representative Hamilton Fish blocked action on bills requiring unanimous consent because his request that the Lindbergh message be put in the Congressional Record was refused.

"As time goes on," Mitchell commented, "you will find those two birds always on the same side of the fence, perhaps in something more serious than this crisis. Lindbergh has disclosed himself as the 'front man' of the Air Trust."

One incident of this affair stirred Mitchell to depths of anger. A sub-committee of the House Military Affairs Committee after secret hearings called upon George H. Dern, Roosevelt's first Secretary of War to oust Major General Benjamin Foulois from his post as Chief of the Air Corps.

Foulois was accused of violating the law in buying airplanes by direct negotiation instead of by competitive bidding. With wanton recklessness the War Department had decided to clear itself of all responsibility for the mail-flying fiasco by unloading all of its incompetency upon a brave man's shoulders. He was accused of making false and misleading statements about Air Corps affairs and blamed directly for the casualties in the ghastly airmail experiment. He was charged with "lying" to the investigating Committee by saying that Army mail pilots had had sufficient night flying experience.

"This is frightful," Mitchell said. "Benny Foulois is the victim of the brass heads. Everybody knows that purchases of airplanes by direct negotiation follow the rule established by the War Department in its dealings with the Air Trust. It's illegal, but it goes right on. No independent companies are allowed to bid. Foulois has to follow the system of the stupid bureaucrats who are trying to chop his head off for their own protection. He's been made the 'goat' after twenty-six years in the service. The Army clique will get him as they got me. I've been flaying this system for years. That's why I'm a private citizen."

Foulois managed to hang on to his post for another year when he "retired" with a brilliant record of devotion to his country. He had drafted the $640,000,000 aviation bill of July 1917 but was in France when the Air Trust manipulators maneuvered successfully to bring about the squandering of the money on the "flaming coffins."

He had been with the Air Corps of the Army when it had consisted of one plane and one pilot in 1908.

"I remember those days," Mitchell said. "Benny operated one of the first planes we had. The Army appropriated $150 for its maintenance. This was only six years before the World War. Benny's first year's repair bills for his plane amounted to $450 and the Army took $300 out of his pocket because the 'brass heads' of the time felt he had spent too much money."

The prominence given in the press to Mitchell's views during the airmail controversy, and his fairly frequent visits to the White House began to cause great uneasiness in both the aircraft industry and in military circles.

More than disquieting to those who opposed him was a report that the White House had scheduled as "must" legislation a bill designed to restore to him all the prerogatives he had surrendered when he resigned from the Air Service. As a matter of fact, such a measure was passed later by the Senate without debate but was to curl up and die in the hands of a committee of his enemies.

Rumors were flying about that the bill was but a first step in a plan by President Roosevelt to set up a Department of Air with the retired General as the virtual czar of all-American aviation. In the War Department, the bureaucrats huddled into conference and sharpened their knives for a fight to the finish against the crusader.

Dern, the Secretary of War, had told an agitated group of Generals, a number of whom had convicted Mitchell, that the unified air plan would go through "over my dead body."

Hatred of the Brigadier General, from the time he had come back from France with a program to solidify and develop the Air Force had become a heritage in the War Department. The Navy could hardly be expected to be any less venomous. The narrow-minded Dern's bitter letter to Senator Morris Sheppard, chairman of the Senate Military Affairs Committee indicated fairly well to the former Air Chief what he might expect in fairness from the "brass heads" still functioning under the New Deal:

"The War Department can find no justification for the enactment of special legislation which would single out Mitchell for preferential treatment from among the many former excellent officers of the regular Army who have voluntarily severed their connection with military service. By voluntary resignation . . . Mitchell forfeited all rights and claims to retirement. This department is firmly of the opinion that he should not be the beneficiary of legislation that would place him in a status that other officers earn by loyal and faithful service."

To add to this insult Dern deliberately twisted the meaning of Mitchell's patriotic phrase which he had humbly addressed to the court-martial in 1925:

"I owe the government everything; the government owes me nothing." Said the Secretary: "This statement accurately reflects the views of the War Department as to the merits of the proposed legislation."

Not long before he died, Dern, perhaps with a touch of remorse, told Representative William I. Sirovich, who was interested in the restoration of Mitchell's prerogatives, that the sentence last quoted had been suggested by a member of the court-martial, who later regretted it himself. As he has since won the Nation's regard his name will not be mentioned here.

Senator Joseph T. Robinson, Democratic Leader of the Senate, who had been using his influence to return Mitchell to the Air Service, believed that the War Department's attitude could be circumvented with the help of the President. The former Air Chief expressed his doubts.

"Joe, it's been that way since the time of Baker, when the whole air scandal began," Mitchell remarked. "I don't know where the Presidents pick these sad antiques, Weeks and all the rest. I expected something from Dern because he's a New Deal man. But these civilian Secretaries, who know nothing about air defense, are poisoned against airplane development as soon as they get into office by the 'brass heads' upon whom they have to depend for information. We're in for it again. Unless the President shakes up the whole General Staff nothing will happen. I'll admit he has plenty of other things on his mind. But protecting the people in case of war is important, too."

The legislation which Robinson had proposed in Mitchell's favor did not call for his return to power and authority in the Air Corps. It was merely to wipe out the stigma under which he had resigned from the Army. It was to make him eligible for retired pay of $375 a month as a colonel with more than thirty years of active service to his credit.

But his enemies were alarmed by the turn of affairs. They pointed out that in his restored status he could, as a colonel, at any time, be called to active duty during the pleasure of the President as Commander-in-Chief of the Army and Navy, and asked to serve in any capacity the President might desire.

The former Air Chief enjoyed ready access to the White House while Robinson fought for his restoration. The fact remains for the records, however, that he had to continue his crusade single-handed as a private citizen until his death.

Between his speech-making trips to awaken the country, Billy Mitchell managed to write another volume about aviation while his children played at his feet in his study at "Boxwood." This time it was Skyways: A Book on Modern Aeronautics. Each year he intended to revise it and print it as the latest compendium on the subject.

It was encyclopedic in scope. He drew upon his recollections of his early experiences and turned out his manuscript with obvious relish. With amusement he described his first "crack-up" on the Potomac. "I knew practically nothing about flying but I made a bad landing which taught me more than anything that ever happened to me in the air." His usual prophecies dominated the book.

"The field for exploration and adventure and things new may be narrowing on the earth's surface. But the air and the sky offer a boundless future to daring spirits that wish to rise into it."

Naturally Mitchell expressed an interest in Pershing's book, My Experiences in the World War, when it finally appeared in the early Thirties. It was one of the last big guns fired in the war of memoirs after the Armistice. The Air Crusader read it thoroughly, at times with a wry expression.

"Well," he said, "that's the way the General sees it. I'm sorry he didn't have more to say about aviation. He fought a good war. But he doesn't know that it will never be fought that way again on this earth. In our present fix, if anything happens, it will be too late for us to say, Lafayette, nous voici!

"One evening at Boxwood, Mitchell threw some interesting light on his activities to fortify Alaska while discussing with Senator Robinson and a newspaper editor, the attitude of the new Secretary of War concerning aviation.

"The vicious letter that Dern wrote to Senator Sheppard explains a number of things to me," he said. "You know I have always believed Alaska to be the most strategic air base on the face of the earth. I have talked to the President about this. You remember how I tried to get Harding started on it. If Japan should ever get Alaska, I am convinced that North America would face the most serious menace since its discovery. A successful Japanese invasion might lead to a gigantic War between the White and the Yellow races if we were caught as we are now. I have been trying for years to get an intelligent Secretary of War to listen to me about my apprehensions. Of course, I can get nowhere with the General Staff.

"I thought when Dern came in that my chance had come and I wrote him a letter with plans, based on years of study, to thwart a Japanese offensive which, I feel sure, would begin along the Aleutians and creep up. This thing will happen when we fight the Japs. It is only a question of time before we will have to fight them. I told Dern that our government should negotiate with Canada to build a highway system to Alaska. A threat from Japan would be of as much importance to the Canadians as it would be to us. We must have a supply line from the United States through Canada to Alaska.

"We need air bases along the way and a gigantic air base in Alaska. We have time to do it if we start now. It will be a tough job because through these stretches there are, in some spots, no signs of solid ground at depths of seventy or eighty feet. It recalls my experiences when I laid telegraph lines down the Yukon for 3,000 miles. Alaska is our most vulnerable spot. Yet, we could use it to dominate the world absolutely. We need scientific aviators to make a study of the Territory immediately. I have in mind men like Jimmy Doolittle.

"We need such men in the Air Force desperately. They will have to be trained to bomb the Japanese out of Alaska—or bomb Japan from Alaska. Aerodynamic experts such as Doolittle should be in the Air Force and required to specialize in the Japanese problems. If we do not chart the waters of Alaska completely, we will live to regret our indifference. Right now, we could build bombers ready to bomb Japan and return to an up to date Alaskan base, in case of eventualities. I figured it all out years ago with a route of supply not too far inland to be used as a line of attack."

"What did Dern say about your letter?" Senator Robinson asked.

"He never answered me," Mitchell replied.

But recognition of Billy Mitchell's theories and exploits came to him at times from quarters which might have surprised his ignorant detractors.

British students of aerodynamics were using his articles as advanced studies. Scientists in England and France met to weigh his predictions. It is significant that Germany developed a keen interest in his conclusions soon after Hitler assumed power.

Mitchell's book, Winged Defense, which had received an official sneer from Major Gullion during the court-martial, and had been called "trash" by the military minstrels who had forced the Air Chief out of the Army, was printed in full by the recognized scientific journal Gasschutz und Luftchutz in Berlin at the end of 1933.

The German editors had the following to say as an introduction to the book on their editorial page:

"In military literature, the name of William Mitchell at present has found no great response in Europe, even much less in America. Notwithstanding the intelligence of the Italians, General Douhet is already widely recognized, and, to great strategists, he is outstanding as a military authority. We must put the American General Mitchell in the same class with Douhet as a forerunner of tremendous vision of the airplane in the history of war. We are compelled to include him with Douhet. Mitchell from now cannot be put aside.

"It is elementary logic to conclude that Douhet would have never been able to expound his theory to the military world had it not been for General Mitchell. "In the German periodicals heretofore, the name of Mitchell has not appeared often enough. The great German people under Der Fuehrer will hear more often, in our publications, about this advanced strategist whose theories in his book, Winged Defense will be invaluable to intelligent people contemplating the future."

Mitchell seldom commented about the attention he was attracting abroad but kept himself particularly well informed of advancements made in German aviation and also of Japanese developments in that branch of warfare.

The name of Douhet, perhaps until Pearl Harbor, would have made as much impression on the majority of the General Staff and the War Department as it would have on an Australian bushman. Yet it was the Douhet theory of aerial warfare which Hitler adopted when he launched his blitzkrieg upon the world.

Soon after Mitchell had startled foreign military experts by sinking a battleship with air bombs, General Giulio Douhet, one-time head of Italy's military aviation, who had corresponded on the subject with Mitchell, announced his theory that a nation could be forced to surrender through systematic destruction of its cities by waves of enemy bombers.

He gave a hypothetical picture of France and Belgium being plowed under in two days by a mighty German air offensive. The Italian General admitted that the safety of civilians would have to be ignored to affect such destruction.

As the war expert Dewitt Mackenzie was to point out in 1942:

"It seemed that Hitler had shown us the limit of bombing possibilities, but two years of bombing have brought great changes, and we now see far more powerful air fleets carrying to German cities the catastrophe of which Douhet dreamed. This is only the beginning of a systematic destruction of German cities, one by one."

Mackenzie might have added that Douhet did not propound his theory until three years after Billy Mitchell had headed the greatest air armada in history up to that time—1,400 airplanes whose air mastery over the Germans had more to do with the "great push" in France than General Pershing was disposed to admit.

That Mitchell's predictions were read extensively in Germany is an established fact from the file of clippings he received from abroad.

German articles treated him with respect, which is a good indication of fear on the part of the Nazis who decorated Lindbergh for less important, if perhaps more insidious, reasons.

Whether Hitler, somewhat of a prophet himself in his book Mein Kampf, read Mitchell's Winged Defense, which warned the world of everything that was to come, is a matter for interesting speculation. It could not have been without his permission or knowledge that his most important aviation magazine referred to Mitchell as the master of Douhet.

By continually looking upwards, Mitchell's mind seemed to grow upwards. Life, he said, had not been given to him for indolent contemplation.

Men of action, he always believed, were nothing but the unconscious instruments of men of thought, but his own thoughts largely prompted his own actions from the time mechanical flight had lifted man from the ground.

His favorite story, which he told, over and over again, had to do with a contrivance of his own invention which had actually lifted him from the ground when he was stringing telegraph wire in Alaska for the Army.

"With the few materials we had at hand," he said, "we made kites, and I found that by putting two large kites in tandem I could evolve a structure that lifted me off the ground. This was long before I learned to fly but it was the most exhilarating experience I ever had. Those kites, by the way, were able to carry wire into the air for over a mile and saved me a lot of work."

Any man-made contraption that could fly was of interest to Mitchell. It was something new. His enthusiasm was by no means confined to airplanes. He was an authority on lighter-than-air craft, hot-air balloons, gas balloons, hydrogen balloons. He had a deep conviction that great dirigibles, properly handled, could be used as aircraft carriers in the sky. He ranked Count Zeppelin with the great leaders of aerodynamics.

"When the gasoline motor was invented in 1879," he would say, "Zeppelin had something to work on. He attached an engine on a ship that could hold the air longer than any other known aircraft. No animal lighter than air has been known to exist on the earth because it would be swept away. This subject has always fascinated me. Once during hunting time, I went down in the Dismal Swamp to study the ballooning spider. Some people said these spiders rose in the air without visible means. With powerful magnifying glasses, I finally found out how they did it. I saw spiders come up and test the air with the sun. They looked like little balloons, but they would throw out almost invisible webs to go up in the air. In a way, that is what we can do with lighter-than-air craft. We can go up in the air whenever we wish, just as the spider does. We can make our own webs, figuratively, and climb on them."

Those who were unfamiliar with Mitchell's experience with lighter-than-air craft may have been surprised to find him as its chief defender when in April 1933, the mighty $8,000,000 dirigible Akron went down in thirty seconds in a storm off Barnegat Lightship. The destruction of the world's greatest airship shocked the country. A large part of the press, whose headlines shrieked with the disaster, turned its files back eight years to recall the catastrophe of the Shenandoah, which still remained in the public mind. Senators and Congressmen were under a deluge of telegrams demanding that dirigibles be abolished.

The usual Committee of Investigation was organized, this time under Senator William H. King of Utah, who was inclined to abolish all lighter-than-air craft as a waste of lives and money. The naval calamity, for such it was in scope for the Bureau of Aeronautics, carried distressing personal significance for Mitchell.

The Akron, the leviathan of the skies, had gone down with Rear Admiral Moffett, who had been his arch-enemy almost from the time of the air bombing of the Ostfriesland. With the Admiral seventy-two brave men had perished, standing calmly at their stations.

Three survivors described Moffett as heroic in death. However, he had flown in defiance of all the warnings the former Air Chief had sounded for years concerning the incompetent handling of airships by the Navy, which apparently believed that experience on warships qualified men to operate above the sea, and persisted in this deadly policy. Under similar circumstances the great dirigible Macon was to be destroyed two years later off the California coast.

Mitchell had nothing to say to the press about his predictions of airship disasters. In "off the record" talks with newspapermen whom he knew, he said, that Moffett had gone to his doom because of his obstinacy. "But he was a brave man," he added, "and, unfortunately, a splendid hater. His bitterness prevented him from listening to me."

Appearing before Senator King's Committee, the retired Air Chief pleaded almost with tears in his eyes to save the airship program. Dirigibles, he said, could be handled by men trained for the purpose. He was certain they could be developed into instruments of incalculable value. His argument carried to his side a majority of the Committee which declined to recommend abolishment of lighter-than-air craft. He could not resist reiterating his oft-expressed wish for a separate Air Service and in an impassioned address evoked laughter from the spectators at the hearing by figuratively—and with gestures—sinking the Navy.

"You think," asked Senator King, "that we are wasting money on battleships?"

"I don't think so; I know it," retorted Mitchell. "The Navy's point of view is different from mine, but an airship can sink anything on top of the water."

He waited to hear the testimony of Colonel Lindbergh who had made an appearance to urge the government to continue its experimental policy in the field of lighter-than-air craft, regardless of the disasters.

Mitchell eyed the "Lone Eagle" curiously and listened closely as the "fair-haired boy" of the aircraft industry delivered his phrases tersely and departed.

Incidentally, the flyer was to receive the main headlines of the hearing.

"That's the first time I've found myself in agreement with him," Mitchell commented. "I always have the feeling, somehow, that he's expressing someone else's opinion."

The General, who was devoting a large part of his time to the task of condensing all available evidence against the Air Trust, for future use against it, openly expressed his disapproval of Lindbergh.

"That boy," he said, "could have done so much for American aviation if he had not been roped in by the monopoly."

In this opinion the crusader found a staunch supporter in Senator George W. Norris of Nebraska, one of the great liberals of the Senate, who had expressed some doubt as to Lindbergh's qualifications as a national idol. Mitchell hoped for an aircraft investigation which might draw more information from Lindbergh than the admissions he had already made for the government records in Congressional hearings.

After his Paris flight, the flyer had become a "front man" for the aircraft industry, a term used by Big Business with no disrespect. Official files in Washington disclosed the story of his financial success plainly enough. Lindbergh had admitted that one aviation company had turned over to him a quarter of a million dollars in cash with an invitation to invest it in its stock. On the records were his admission that he had made profits from dealings in that stock totaling nearly $200,000.

He admitted, according to record of his testimony, that another aviation company furnished him with warrants to buy its stock, from which he profited to the extent of more than $150,000 and that both companies and a railroad which, for some reason not fully explained, was interested in aviation, each put him on the payroll at $10,000 a year as technical adviser.

Aside from the profits made from aviation stocks with money that was pushed his way to play on surefire Wall Street aviation tips, he had an annual salary of $30,000. All this he had admitted in his testimony.

Mitchell, studying this record, grinned: "That boy is not going to testify against the Air Trust."

What the air crusader would have said, had he lived long enough to learn that Lindbergh had been decorated in Berlin by the Nazis and had returned to America to lead the "America First" group in a program of suicidal isolationism up to Pearl Harbor, is something which the authors will leave for the reader to speculate upon.

For a time after his appearance in the Akron investigation, Mitchell vanished from the headlines under circumstances of his own choice. Close friends who saw him at "Boxwood" said he was loading his guns. They were well loaded, as the public discovered when, a few weeks after his disappearance, he turned his heaviest artillery upon the leading companies of the Air Trust.

The occasion for his declaration of war was a luncheon of the Foreign Policy Association at the Astor in New York.

Mentioning by name all companies and banks involved in the aircraft monopoly he accused them of having sidetracked safety for greed. The withering speech which had seldom been equaled in the seriousness of its charges against a business combination was widely printed and carried in detail in The New York Times.

"I'll hear from that one," he remarked, with his chin out, as he sat down.

His predictions were correct. His address brought immediate repercussions. A suit demanding damages of $250,000 on the charge of libel was brought against him by the companies he had mentioned before he could leave the city. He accepted the service of the papers with defiance.

"That's the first attempt to muzzle me as a citizen," he said. "Now the fight is on to the end. The real fight."

Soon the radio was carrying Mitchell's commanding voice over the land:

"The Air Force ... our first arm of defense. We must build it up!"

"It must be a United Air Force..."

"Battleships are doomed..."

"A Secretary of Defense..."

"More planes! Better planes!"

"New York must protect itself."

Mitchell seemed to be everywhere. A New York newspaper editor (co-author of this book) received that impression far out on the Atlantic, on board the aircraft carrier Saratoga, which was taking part in attack maneuvers in a lashing storm of rain and hail. Far up on a deck on the side turret from which he could see planes roaring off to sea, the newspaperman felt a tap on his shoulder.

He turned to confront a muffled figure in oilskins and rubber hat. It was Mitchell, with his old-time cordial grin. The editor had known him since the days of the court-martial.

"I'm the phantom," the air crusader laughed. "I'm the phantom of the Navy. I got an invitation to attend this demonstration from Secretary Swanson as a writer. You might call me an expert. Let's go below. I want to show you a few things."

Down in the magazine he pointed to the ammunition stores.

"What do you suppose would happen," he asked, "if a bomber dropped one of its pills on us right now? All the planes are gone from our deck. We are defenseless. If we were hit in this section we'd explode and go down like a Mack truck. Years ago, I was inclined to believe the carrier might solve our sea problem. But I should never have deviated from my first theory. The carrier is as vulnerable as the battleship. The dreadnaught will be the first to pass out of the picture. Carriers will then fight it out with their planes until we realize that there are only two dominating instruments of war left to us: the long-distance bomber and the submarine."

From the turret, again he studied the massive hulk of the Lexington which had loomed out of a thick, purple smoke screen like an apparition, to receive her returning planes. The two carriers were halted off the Virginia Capes.

"God, what a target," he exclaimed, his eyes glued on the Lexington. "Imagine what fifty planes would do to that floating mass with aerial torpedoes. One square hit would be enough. Carriers are not the answer. Bombers must be built to fight from land bases, no matter what the distance may be from the objective. That will come. Great bombers with tremendous range will answer all purposes of attack. Carriers are just floating airdromes. A plane that has to stay home to protect its base, and in the ocean, of all places, will not be worth much in offensive work. What happens to the plane when the base goes down?"

The answer was to come eight years later when, after the great carrier Lexington had been sent to the bottom of the Coral Sea, its brave commander, Captain Frederick Carl Sherman, said: "No offensive force can stop a determined air force."

The planes were swooping down at a stiff angle through murky weather upon the decks of the Saratoga, their movement arrested almost at the landing point by hooks which, hanging from the machines, were caught by steel cables of surprising elasticity that held them fast while propellers turned slower and slower and finally stopped like dying pinwheels without a breeze.

The landing mechanism seemed to fascinate Mitchell who lay on his stomach on the deck in the rain in order to watch its operations more closely.

"Ingenious," he agreed, "but that's a hell of a tug on the plane. It shakes it all up."

Pilots, some of them mere boys, it seemed, were scrambling out of their open cabins, their eyes shining with the sporting pleasure of their sham battle. The word flashed about that the former Air Chief was on deck.

"That's Mitchell! That's Mitchell!"

As he was getting to his feet, a number of flyers gathered about him. A smiling redheaded youngster, his face beaming, grasped his hand. "I hope our show suits you, General. We're doing our best," the boy said.

Mitchell shook hands with many and patted some of them on the back. He watched them almost wistfully as they ran and skipped to their quarters, horse-playing on the deck, like schoolboys going home, forgetting their planes which were pushed to the elevator deck by breathless mechanics.

"Grand boys!" The General shook his head, his eyes following them. "By God, the nation should be proud of them. They'll save the country."

Soon the masses of planes had been lowered on the elevator and disappeared under the deck cover.

"They're all bunched together down there now," Mitchell pointed. "One big bomb would finish them. On a field, during an attack, planes would be scattered, or up in the air, fighting. No, this is not the solution. We've got to get the idea out of our heads that we're protecting battleships with planes. It's the country that we've got to protect."

He climbed up to the Captain's lookout through the rain which had begun again, whipped by a briny wind that slashed the face like little blades. He had to poise at the railing, breathing hard, and pressed his heart.

"Boats were never made for me, anyhow," he muttered.

He joined a group of strategists around the Captain. There had been some excitement as the maneuvers closed. One of the pilots had failed to return and Mitchell, hearing of it, quickly pushed through the ring of officers.

"Have you heard from the boy?" he snapped. "Is he all right?"

"Yes," the Captain said.

He seemed relieved.

"He's all right, General. He had to land in Virginia. He had us worried a bit. Something wrong with the engine."

Mitchell asked about the carrier's position and led the editor to the rail where the Lexington ploughed ahead, destroyers playing around her like dolphins.

"We're sixty miles off the Capes," he said. He wiped his face in the rain, his features developing the two deep perpendicular lines on each side of his mouth, characteristic of him when he cast his mind back. "According to the Captain's reckoning," he added slowly, "we're right over the spot where I sank the Ostfriesland thirteen years ago."

Mitchell's plan of campaign to expose the aircraft monopoly had been developed to far-reaching proportions when the editor saw him again in Washington. The General had induced Representative William I. Sirovich, chairman of the Committee on Patents of the House of Representatives, to introduce a bill in Congress which called for legislation to end all patent-pooling arrangements affecting industry. It was directed at the heart of the system under which the Air Trust had been operating since the first World War.

"If this bill can be made into law," said Mitchell, almost trembling with the idea which possessed him, "we will free the government from the worst combination that has ever gripped it. We will be able to have the right kind of planes. The country's safety is behind this."

He became as stern as a general on the eve of battle as his plan unfolded. The Committee on Patents had the power to investigate and summon by subpoenas signed by the Speaker of the House all leaders of the Air Trust. They would be put on the stand. They would be shaken down. They would have to answer all questions about the sustained evidence which for years had been buried in government files about the "billion-dollar air conspiracy," concerning which nothing had ever been done. Records would have to be produced to reveal the sales of airplanes to foreign powers.

The country would wake up when it realized what was happening. Investigators would have to be carefully chosen under the direction of a man who knew how to dig up facts.

"That's where you come in," Mitchell told the editor (who had already been approached on the subject by Representative Sirovich). "You're going to be appointed director-in-chief of the investigation. You couldn't tackle a more patriotic job. The President knows what we're going to do. I've been working on this for months. I've gathered some brave witnesses; my old friend, Jimmy Martin, the inventor, for one. His inventions were all stolen through the pool. He's had to close his factory because he wouldn't join the Trust. He's the father of most of the basic inventions used on airplanes today. He started out with me. He'll take the stand with me. He has great courage. He's the man, you'll remember, who refused to make the 'flaming coffins.' He's been hounded ever since. What a story he has to tell!

"If you like adventure you'll get all the thrills your constitution can stand. We're going after a tough crowd. You'll be followed around by foreign spies and you'll have to watch your step. I've warned Sirovich about this. I'll fire the first gun with my testimony to warn the Nation. In the meantime, I'll supply you with all the leads. You'll have to follow through. You'll have to carry one end of the load. Do you like it?"

The editor liked it.

14 - A PROPHET TALKS FOR THE RECORD

Testimony of Brigadier General William Mitchell, United States Army, re-
tired, before the Committee on Patents, House of Representatives,
investigating the pooling of patents of American aircraft industries, February
1935. Hon. William I. Sirovich presiding as Chairman.

General Mitchell. Well, here I am again, Gentlemen, with my old story. I've been telling it to the Congress for seventeen years.

The Chairman. I think we can find the time you want for your statement. Proceed, General.

General Mitchell. We are at the mercy of an aircraft industry which has pooled its patents and can do what it pleases with its products. Remember, Gentlemen, that national defense in the next war will be measured primarily by air power, because a military threat against a country must be against its population and re-sources, not against its army and navy. A navy exerts its power through blockade. The aircraft attached to a navy are merely for the protection of the navy, not for the protection of the country.

The Chairman. A strong statement, General. Explain it a bit more.

General Mitchell. A navy acts in an indecisive theater and is subject to comparatively easy destruction at the hands of aircraft. As long as a navy exists, of course it will have to have suitable aircraft for its protection. An army can only advance to the centers of popu-lation and resources over the land, by such a slow and laborious process that it is becoming almost impossible on account of the de-velopment of missile throwing and chemical weapons.

The Chairman. Do you mean to say that aircraft will dominate all arms of defense?

General Mitchell. I mean that aircraft can go straight to their destination no matter where that may be. Nothing known at present can stop them. The recent defensive agreement between France and England specifies that in case of certain eventualities in Europe, they will combine their air forces for striking at an enemy's popula-tion and resources. No mention is made of an army or navy, because these act in indecisive theaters. The air is the decisive theater.

The Chairman. How does that apply to this country?

General Mitchell. Your hearing on the pooling of aircraft patents answers that question. Why should the United States be prevented from developing this priceless attribute, the airplane, for our national defense in which we are entirely capable of excelling, through our initiative, inventive ability, raw materials, industrial developments, and the personal characteristics of our people?

In reality, it is our basic means of national defense. The aircraft monopoly, with its ramifications, its influence and its practices, is a serious menace to the future of our country. We keep having investigations and boards which lead to practically nothing. These have developed no change in policy or system. These boards have been directly influenced by the aircraft monopoly for years. Consequently, none of them have directly recommended against the pooling of patents; on the other hand, they have recommended the purchase of aircraft (by the government) by negotiation instead of open bidding, which is merely another means of establishing a monopoly, reducing the number of manufacturers and whacking up the money between a favored few.

The Chairman. How much was spent for aircraft during the World War?

General Mitchell. The gigantic sum of $1,650,000,000.

The Chairman. You say the ships made then killed more men than the Germans did.

General Mitchell. Yes; in the air and on our training fields since the war.

The Chairman. In other words, it is your contention we have not a single ship at the present time capable of combating foreign countries?

General Mitchell. We couldn't fight a first-class country in the air. That is a fact. It is not a contention.

The Chairman. Please elaborate on this subject, General.

General Mitchell. I can only repeat what I have said for seventeen years. The money appropriated for our aircraft has fallen into the hands of a few financial manipulators who in some instances have boosted their stock from $1 to $10,000 a share, enriching themselves and their associates. The American people were taxed for this money. Congress appropriated it and the aircraft was developed with government money. If there were any profit from this it should have accrued to the people, not to a few financial manipulators.

It can be shown that these manipulators gained control of our aircraft industry (if it can be called such, being entirely supported by the government) during the World War; that agents, associates, friends, or hirelings of these people have continued to manipulate it ever since, except for about five years after the war, when they were run to cover by those of us who returned from the campaign in Europe.

However, the Morrow board, in 1925, put them in control again, and each year since, initiative in aeronautical matters has been stifled more and more, together with invention, development and progress. If this thing is allowed to continue, Gentlemen, it will become more of a scandal and disgrace to the country than anything we have ever had in the past. It will cost us human lives by the thousands. It will make it necessary for us, in case of war, to depend on foreigners for our aircraft, our vital means of defense. That is where you would have to go today to get them if we had a war.

The Chairman. Develop that statement further, General.

General Mitchell. Today, United States service engines, the heart of our aircraft, are practically monopolized by two firms. The largest engines they make are about 750 to 800 horsepower. These are ordinary gas engines. In Europe, Diesel engines are now flying in aircraft. Gas engines up to 3,000 horsepower (I hope these figures impress you, Gentlemen) are being made and have been made already in Europe.

Our potential enemies have superchargers which give their service aircraft a ceiling of 35,000 feet or more. There is no necessity for our being left in the lurch. If the United States would provide a personnel of public servants dedicated primarily to the development of air power, not to the Army or Navy or the airplane monopoly, we would get somewhere, as we have proved in the past, but it cannot be done under present conditions.

The Chairman. You believe our aircraft production is completely in the hands of a trust?

General Mitchell. We need a great number of responsible bidders for aircraft designs. Instead of that we have a few large companies in control. By having a great number of small factories, we would get more competition. Last year, when the Army desired to get some competition for bombers, there was only one firm that could make them according to Army specifications. This was a bomber of such short range of operation that it is now unsuitable for modern war. The officers in the armed services who know about aviation are so suppressed and coerced by their non-flying superiors that it is usually impossible, as the Military Committee of this House of Representatives will tell you, to get open, free and uninfluenced opinions from them. The result is that merchants of aircraft and financial manipulators are getting away with murder, literally and figuratively, by killing pilots and passengers.

The Chairman. Why do you think this condition continues?

General Mitchell. Our boards of investigation take the word of lobbyists of the interests who testify how wonderful American equipment is, how superior to anything in the world. The people who know this is not so do not dare to testify. The number of world records held by us right now is a good indication of our status. Out of ninety-six world records recognized by the International Federation of Aeronautics, the United States holds less than ten. After the war, when I had control of Army aviation, we held practically all the world's records.

The Chairman. You believe monopoly has choked competition?

General Mitchell. Henry Ford is a good example of it. He had one of the best equipped airplane factories in this country and turned out excellent equipment, but he would not join the monopoly. He was then so harassed by it that he had to close his factory. This was only two years ago, in 1933.

The Chairman. Does the monopoly traffic with foreign powers?

General Mitchell. The factories of the monopoly are open under certain restrictions to the agents of foreign powers. As the government has no control over the manufacturers, any secrets might very easily leak out as we do not have a strong enough Espionage Act to punish people working on government supplies for revealing whatever they know about them. That condition does not apply in other countries.

The Chairman. You believe our present system is wasting the people's money?

General Mitchell. Ninety million dollars is being asked by the Army for airplanes this year, and the Navy will probably ask for a like amount. There being no united aeronautical service in this country, the overhead will eat up that money and methods opposed to each other will be used by the Army and Navy. What is the use of taking public money and pouring it into the laps of these manufacturers for a lot of airplanes that will be worse than worthless to us in war? Numbers mean nothing in the air. It is excellence and suitability that count quality, not quantity. Do you realize, Gentlemen, that some of our great aeronautical engineers have practically nothing to do now? Excellent aircraft developed by smaller manufacturers have been limited by the engines available and by the stupid service requirements of the Army. The equipment we need is not being turned out.

The Chairman. Should the recent Balbo flight bear special significance to us?

General Mitchell. That Italian flight to the United States was made with 1,500-horsepower engines stepped down to 950-horsepower. Our own first pursuit group could not have kept up with these flying boats. If the United States had a group of 200 bombers right now, with a radius of action of 6,000 miles, each capable of carrying two or three tons of bombs, the debt question in Europe might not be so difficult of solution. And bear in mind that there would be no trouble in the Pacific. We have been able to build such ships for several years, but have never done it, due directly to the opposition of the Army.

All these things were foreseen and provided for, and experimentation was started in 1919 and 1920 when we came back from the European war. The stopping by the Army of this great development program for American aviation, I predict, within a few years, will constitute one of the darkest pages in the military history of this country. Bombers such as those I mention would cost about $300,000. As I recall it, the foreign debts due us are something like $12,000,000,000.

The Chairman. From the appropriation of $1,650,000,000 for aircraft during the last war how many planes were built?

General Mitchell. Roughly, around 12,000.

The Chairman. Were they sent over during the war?

General Mitchell. All I got as Chief of the Air Force in France was 196 of them. The rest were junked or saved and many of them unloaded by the Air Trust on the Russians after the revolution. They were the worst planes that possibly could have been built. They could not have been any worse.

The Chairman. Were the airplanes manufactured in this country during the last war inferior to the machines of other countries?

General Mitchell. Yes, but it was not due to the fact that our industry was not capable. We could have equaled the quality of any airplane in the world.

The Chairman. Why did we turn out inferior planes?

General Mitchell. Because the monopoly obtained control of aircraft production in this country and shifted the business to its own factories. The Hughes committee went all over this matter and ordered the court-martial of those responsible.

The Chairman. What happened then?

General Mitchell. Nothing.

The Chairman. Does the monopoly today include in its membership the leading manufacturers of airplanes?

General Mitchell. It includes ninety-eight per cent of them. There are one or two outsiders. Most of them have been forced into it.

The Chairman. Who was one on the outside?

General Mitchell. Major Alexander P. de Seversky, one of the most capable experts in aerodynamics in this country. If he is not choked by the combination, he will perform a great service to America.

The Chairman. Is it possible for a manufacturer who is not a member of the patent-pool monopoly to build successfully competitive airplanes without negotiating for the various patents controlled by the Trust?

General Mitchell. The monopoly claims that it cannot be done. Airplane patents are in the hands of the few. Outsiders fear that if they construct aircraft, they will be forced to join the monopoly and surrender to it what they consider valuable patents of their own. They know that if they refuse to join, they will be forced into destructive litigation. The case of Fleet, Consolidated, occurs to me. This company made fine pursuit airplanes. It was headed by R. H. Fleet, a former officer in the Army who wanted to hold out like Ford did by refusing to throw his patents into the trust's pool. He fought to the last ditch, submerged by eleven suits for alleged infringements. At that time, he was badly injured in an airplane crash and in order to avoid further trouble he joined the monopoly on the advice of the directors of his company.

Mr. (Fritz G.) Lanham. Is this such a monopoly as can be handled through the Department of Justice?

General Mitchell. Yes. Even without further legislation the Federal Trade Commission, with the help of the Department of Justice, could ask for a Federal injunction to stop these practices. Mr. (Charles) Kramer. I think there is a statute that releases anyone that may be building airplanes for the government.

The Chairman. That is a law of 1917 or 1918, enacted during the war and that has never been rescinded. You have told the press that a bomber of our Air Force today has a range of about 1,000 miles, 500 going and 500 to come back.

General Mitchell. Yes, for a bomber.

The Chairman. You have stated that bombers can go up from 23,000 to 35,000 feet.

General Mitchell. I have said that the foreigners can go up 35,000 feet. We can only reach 23,000 feet.

The Chairman. Do you think that if we were not harassed by the monopoly that we could build a bomber with a range of 4,000 miles to go across the Pacific and come back?

General Mitchell. I know it; I do not merely think so. We could build such ships at the present time. We do not have anything like that, now.

The Chairman. Is it a fact that foreign countries could develop such machines, capable of going out at any time to attack the United States by flying 35,000 feet up, above the clouds, and through their knowledge of astronomy determine their position over the earth and drop explosive bombs that would destroy our cities?

General Mitchell. Yes.

The Chairman. And we could do nothing against them?

General Mitchell. No.

The Chairman. For our own good, according to your statements, we need ships capable of flying great distances.

General Mitchell. Yes, exactly. We must remember that our immediate problem is in the Pacific. If Japan seizes Alaska, she can take New York.

The Chairman. In other words, if Japan could seize the Aleutian Islands, she could use them as a base, bomb the whole Pacific and destroy Hawaii.

General Mitchell. In that case Japan would not pay any attention to Hawaii. If she had the airplane bombers, we describe she would go straight to New York.

The Chairman. How long would it take to go from Alaska to New York with one of these fast bombers?

General Mitchell. Those ships would have a load speed of 160 to 200 miles an hour. It would take them twenty hours to reach New York.

The Chairman. Up in the air at 35,000 feet where no one could see them?

General Mitchell. They would not have to go that high, but they should have that ceiling. They are building ships designed for that purpose.

The Chairman. Do we have any Diesel engines in any of our bombers and pursuits?

General Mitchell. Those engines are among the problems we do not recognize at all in this country. We still stick to the old ideas of the Army, the way it was during the bombings on the Western Front in 1918, keeping within 250 miles of the supplies. Now in 1935, we call that 'defense' when long distance planes are being made abroad to attack the population and reserves. Our Army has never allowed the development of the long-distance bomber. We must have bombers which can jump a long way and jump back, and we should have, as soon as we possibly can, subterranean air bases where our airplanes could be put, with deposits for fuel, facilities for making repairs. These planes could then get out quickly and prevent bombardment. The Italians, for instance, have a regular factory inside the Alps. They have a hydroelectric plant underground that is impregnable.

Such places are as gas-tight as they can be. The officers' quarters are apartments, invisible from the air but with gas-tight plateglass windows from which observers can see around the country. These places are so cleverly constructed that they take on the appearance of the natural topography. The Germans have twenty-one of these places. Japan has them, going clear through mountains so that airplanes can come in on each side. Our potential enemies have these things.

The Chairman. I understand that the Germans have almost perfected a secret weapon, a peculiar ray that can stop the engine of any airplane in the air except a Diesel engine. Is that true?

General Mitchell. The Germans were working on that invention during the last war. Since then many people have tackled the same problem. We have tried to do something of the kind here, although it is kept a secret. I know that our own ray can follow an engine the distance of this long room. But the amount of power necessary to send it far in the air has not been developed through this invention. It is something that causes a continuous spark and makes it impossible for an engine to operate. The Germans, around their frontier, have a group of fouling stations that cause gasoline ignition, to be used against non-Diesel planes. Diesel engines, which do not take the spark, are not affected. Diesels are more economical for air operation.

Mr. Kramer. Can Diesel planes carry as much fuel as other machines?

General Mitchell. Rather more than one and a half times as much gas. In other words, a Diesel plane has double the radius of operation of a non-Diesel.

The Chairman. Could searchlights detect invading planes 23,000 to 35,000 feet up in a night attack?

General Mitchell. You cannot stop an attack.

The Chairman. Then, according to your statement, any of our large cities today would be at the mercy of long-distance bombers, such as we are discussing.

General Mitchell. Yes, they would be subject to attack.

The Chairman. We do not have such ships in our country.

General Mitchell. No.

The Chairman. What percentage of American aircraft made by the monopoly goes to foreign countries?

General Mitchell. Between seventy and eighty percent.

The Chairman. Foreign countries are getting our secrets?

General Mitchell. I do not know that we have any secrets. A foreigner can buy his way into any plant where aircraft is made in this country under the monopoly. The government has no control over it. An agent can find out exactly the progress we are making. Secrets do not matter, apparently. We are selling our engines outright to the Japanese. I know we sold plenty of them last year.

Mr. Kramer. Is it not a fact that the Japanese are employing the men that made those planes and acquired our information that way?

General Mitchell. The Japanese are buying our planes and are buying the right to manufacture them under license from our monopoly.

Mr. Kramer. They employed some of the men we did?

General Mitchell. Yes.

Mr. (Scott W.) Lucas. If your theory is correct that there should be independent aircraft manufacture, and the Army is against that theory, isn't it a fact that whatever is done in that direction will have no particular effect on the Army?

General Mitchell. If we did away with the pool of patents and opened the aircraft business to everyone, it would increase the incentive to inventors to a great degree. Creative men are forced out. I have in mind right now, Gentlemen, five skillful engineers, one of whom is reduced to making zippers for shoes; another is grinding valves on engines. A few of them have been able to get jobs in the Department of Commerce.

Mr. Lanham. It is hard to understand how an officer of the Army, upon whom we rely primarily for defense and protection, could be so forgetful of the interests of his country as to permit the construction of airplanes inferior to those of other nations. Are such men absolutely ignorant of aviation?

General Mitchell. They are bound hand and foot by the General Staff.

Mr. Lanham. That is just one step removed from the Chief of Staff of the Army?

General Mitchell. It is just through ignorance of the class of equipment that is prescribed. There has always been a question whether the government should control a few large aircraft organizations, so long as it supports them, as it is now doing, or whether we should have many small companies, competing with each other to give us something new.

Mr. (Thomas) O'Malley. Is it not true that where there is an absolute monopoly of a certain group of patents, the manufacturers in control keep putting out old, outworn equipment because it is cheaper than to develop these patents as machinery would have to be changed? Isn't that why they keep selling us old engines for aircraft instead of putting out more money for new engines in experimental ships?

General Mitchell. That is exactly what has been happening for years. If you will investigate this thing you will find out how it has been put over on the people—old stuff of inferior quality sold to the government, simply to keep the combination going.

The Chairman. The airplane industry has been established by the profit motive. The government is trying through a subsidy, to finally perfect airplanes for this country. We have certain models of various engines we would like to try out, but the monopoly wants to maintain the models already in use because experimentation costs money. That's the proposition!

General Mitchell. Such practices are controlled in Europe by governments which subsidize factories but keep control of them by owning a majority of the stock. That is how they obtain aircraft development. If you leave it to a factory it will not change its methods because that is an expensive process. That is why, in this country, two companies have a complete monopoly of service engines.

The Chairman. From secret information that you have, is Japan better equipped with airplanes than we are?

General Mitchell. Of course.

The Chairman. What is the cruising radius of the Japanese?

General Mitchell. The Japanese are trying to conceal such information, but I think they now have airplanes that cruise 3,500 miles. The Russians have, too, and the Russian ships make 3,500 miles and carry two tons of bombs.

Mr. Kramer. Have the Japanese improved the engines which they bought from our country?

General Mitchell. The Japanese use them for purposes of experimentation and other reasons, some of them being commercial. They did buy these engines from our country.

Mr. Kramer. The planes that were sent to you during the war, when we spent that $1,650,000,000, were not even able to cope with the private planes that were manufactured then, were they?

General Mitchell. No.

Mr. Kramer. Why did the government continue to take all this junk off someone's hands?

General Mitchell. That has all been shown in the investigations. A group of manipulators got control of our aircraft, that crowd from Ohio, and spread the stuff around just as they wanted to.

Mr. Kramer. They loaded the government up with junk that they knew was inferior when the United States was at war?

General Mitchell. I can show you the recommendations I sent to our government on the 22nd of April 1917. We had a very short time to get on the job.

Mr. Kramer. Did you know that the planes they sent you in France were of no value before they were shipped?

General Mitchell. Yes.

Mr. Kramer. Why did you take them?

General Mitchell. We had to take them.

Mr. Kramer. What were the names of the ships that were sent to you?

General Mitchell. We had to fight with only one kind of ship, the DH-4 with the Liberty engine.

Mr. Kramer. Was that the "flaming coffin?" Who manufactured it?

General Mitchell. The "flaming coffin" was manufactured all over the country in a great many different plants. The gang had trouble trying to give it out to various plants, but they had to build them.

Mr. O'Malley. Were many of our pilots killed in those machines?

General Mitchell. A great many.

The Chairman. In the training at Fort Worth, fourteen men out of every 100 were killed in fifty hours' flight.

General Mitchell. That is close to it.

Mr. Kramer. Pooling of patents has been going on in the United States and nothing has been done except investigations.

General Mitchell. That is all that was ever done. The whole country knows the truth of what I say.

Mr. Lucas. What about our airplanes for commercial purposes?

General Mitchell. They are not safe enough. These ships ought to be equipped with cabin parachutes to permit the passengers to get out. Automatic pilots should be on board, a lot of things. Ships are not sufficiently developed without these improvements.

The Chairman. You spoke of a stock going up from $1 to $10,000 when the manipulators got into the aircraft business. What is that stock worth today?

General Mitchell. I don't know. I think it's around $9 now. That's all in the Black committee report. It was boosted from $23 to $35,000,000.

The Chairman. Raised to how much?

General Mitchell. I said $35,000,000. William E. Boeing's original investment, for instance, was $487.19. He ran that up to $30,000,000. He received $853,372 of the stock of the United Aircraft, actually taking the profits, a little over $12,000,000 and had 36,000 shares left on hand.

The Chairman. All those facts have been developed before the Black committee?

General Mitchell. That is the report of the Black committee based on the evidence. For instance, one company sold stock to the monopoly. The only money the monopoly got in was what went through the combination which had to pay $6,000,000 to the bankers to get $13,000,000 into the treasury to take care of obligations, the whole thing amounting to over $75,000,000.

The Chairman. You mean that $6,000,000 in interest was paid to the bankers on a $13,000,000 loan? Interest or a commission?

General Mitchell. Just a boost. That was their commission. The Black committee report has it all down.

The Chairman. Have the Japanese any lighter-than-air craft?

General Mitchell. I should think they have. They got one ship at the end of the Armistice and took it to pieces and studied it. They have ships similar to that one. They are well constructed, strategic ships to keep near the coast or around the islands that are between Honolulu and Japan and the islands of Alaska.

Mr. Lanham. There are rumors that the Japanese have got helium in volcanic gases.

General Mitchell. They've looked for everything in Manchuria where they have oil and rock. They've examined the rock to get oil.

Mr. Lucas. Do you think they are even looking for us?

General Mitchell. I do not know.

Mr. Lucas. Does our Navy Department realize what our need is?

General Mitchell. We should speed up the development of everything in aerodynamics, including lighter-than-air craft. The Navy is not doing it, neither is the Army because they are behind the times. The Regular Army is studying about the Mexican War, the Revolutionary War and the World War. The Navy is concerned with the idea of following the fleet. It is working on the idea of servicing the fleet, otherwise no Navy.

Mr. Lucas. We should have an independent Air Force?

General Mitchell. That is the way everyone in the world has it. With an independent Air Force all this "monkey business" would be gotten rid of, pooling of patents, and not having any aircraft to go to war with at once. We need the continuous training of competent officers for the air, but we have to depend on the Army and Navy, ingrained with the psychology that the Navy governs the water by bringing about a blockade through the stomach and that the Army has the hostile main force as its objective.

The Air Force should not be tied to this theory. The Army can only see the battlefield in front of it, just five miles in front of its face. It can't move. It has been in a state of arrested development ever since the last war.

Mr. Lucas. The air forces of the other powers, I take it, are not under the authority of the Army and Navy?

General Mitchell. We are the only ones. The Japanese have a naval air service but a very good one. They can go to Nagasaki in foggy weather and they have very good stuff (planes).

Mr. Lanham. Would an independent Air Force eliminate jealousy and prejudice between the branches of defense?

General Mitchell. It would stop it. If we had a department of national defense, the Army would defend the land, the Navy the sea and the Air Force, the air. We had no trouble in Europe when Admiral Beatty headed the sea and Foch, the land. If we had combined our Air Force in 1919, after the Armistice, I would have commanded it and we would have had no trouble. The way we are doing things today in this country, we are simply organizing for defeat and spending more money on our national services than any country in the world; just organizing for defeat.

The thick-headedness of our Regular Army... and I have served on the General Staff and been all through it... is something remarkable. We tried to get artillery before the last war but when we got into it, everything we had was not our own. Even now. The rifles we fought with were Mausers, a German weapon. The artillery was a French weapon. I went through the Spanish war with a 45-caliber Springfield on my back. The Indians must have had better equipment.

Mr. Lucas. The Army does not agree with you that it is thick-headed.

General Mitchell. It's thick-headed because it has not developed a thing. That's the reason it disagrees with me. It must be that.

The Chairman. Even in legislation some of the people in Congress are twenty years behind the times. Those who protest against economic conditions are called radicals, Bolsheviks, communists. It's a matter of educating the public.

General Mitchell. I will have to say this about the Army. I was in it. There has never been a better instrument of government in this country than the Regular Army, as far as its constitution and history allow it to be. West Point offers wonderful training; but in every one of our contests, history shows that in a crisis, the needed man came from the outside. He has either come from civil life or has returned to the Army after serving in it. General Lee, General Grant and General Sherman are examples of this. If you remain in the Army you become stupefied with routine. You begin to believe there is a written answer for everything, like turning to paragraph 6, section 2 for a quick solution in case something happens. All this has its value as far as a national constabulary is concerned.

But it does not develop anything new and there is no use in trying to tell you that anything new will come out of it. You know the Army's attitude every time the question of establishing an Air Service in the country comes up. The Army fell down in carrying the air mail. All it could do was to call for a board of investigation. Just another board. All the boards have been just the same; long, narrow and wooden.

I can write the opinions of these boards before they meet. You should be tired of executive boards telling you what to do. Do it here in legislation!

What can boards decide about national defense? The people all over the country are becoming impressed with the fact that we will have to defend ourselves because the world is six times smaller than it was. It is simply one-sixth as big as it was at the time of the Spanish War. I am close to the people and there is no use in not talking plainly to them.

There is no trouble about our people. I have watched our boys in the battle-line, and they have done wonders. I still remember what our raw troops did in the Philippines.

15 - THE OLD INVENTOR'S WARNING

Testimony of the inventor James V. Martin of the Martin Airplane Factory at Garden City, Long Island, before the Committee on Patents, House of Representatives, investigating the pooling of patents of American aircraft industries, February-March 1935. Hon. William I. Sirovich, presiding as chairman.

THE CHAIRMAN. I WILL CALL NOW one of our most distinguished inventors, Mr. James V. Martin; one of the great pioneers in the aircraft industry.

Mr. Martin. I have been appearing at these hearings since the Hughes investigation eighteen years ago. You know about me. I don't have to take up your time by introducing myself.

The Chairman. We will interrogate you as you go on. Proceed.

Mr. Martin. My first recommendation would be that we have a real investigation of the Air Trust. You know who the members are of the combination. I was a witness before Judge Hughes, the present Chief Justice, who recommended them for criminal indictment and prosecution. Nothing was done about it. Senator Hugo Black's report has brought the whole matter up again.

The Chairman. Do you realize that one of those you have mentioned at this hearing as a monopoly man was Chief of Aerodynamics and worked under General Mitchell? You are accusing one of the most brilliant men the government had. He devised a valuable instrument and when he had perfected it the Combination took him away from the government. He is now general manager of one of the plants of the monopoly.

Mr. Martin. I knew the gentleman when he was working for the War Department at Dayton, Ohio. He is the same man who is now passing the material through to Japan. Japan has an avenue for acquiring information as to all of our best military and naval secrets through the Air Trust.

Mr. Lanham. Can Mr. Martin continue his statement at our next meeting?

Mr. Martin. You think I will be here for the next meeting?

The Chairman. What do you think might happen to you?

Mr. Martin. There are a great many things that have been gotten away with for much less. I have no personal fear, but I have almost given up hope of justice after this eighteen-year old conspiracy which is ten times worse than Teapot Dome.

The Chairman. For the benefit of the record I call your attention, Mr. Martin, to the fact that you are accusing the monopoly directly of serious crimes, from murder down, against those who have been opposed to it in the past. Do you wish to have that statement in the record?

Mr. Martin. Yes. I have documents to back up my charges. I have been connected with fourteen prominent investigations in eighteen years and they have either been curtailed prior to complete disclosures or else they have been completely taken over by agents of the Air Trust. You must make sure, this time, that your investigation is in the hands of brave men. This is a matter of vast consequence. Hundreds of millions of dollars have been literally stolen from the people. I have a record here which shows that twenty millions of dollars have passed through the monopoly without the government getting five cents in return. Last year, before the Military Affairs Committee, I had documents to verify that seventy-five cents out of every dollar appropriated for aircraft was being stolen. There has been no improvement. The independent companies are now completely crushed out.

The Chairman. Before we adjourn, we will give you a chance to have all the testimony put into the record that you are willing to offer.

Mr. Martin. Of all the old pioneers who started in the aircraft business years ago, fifty-three are left who appeared in 1925 before the Lampert committee, fifty-three witnesses who will verify my charges. We have all been forced out of business. My factory is probably the only one left, and that is not running. It is closed down.

The Chairman. How long has it been closed?

Mr. Martin. For seven or eight years so far as any airplane work is concerned, although documents incorporated under oath by the leaders of the Army and Navy

Design and Aeronautics Section show that my designs for from sixty to one hundred models were accepted, new features of design that were thoroughly approved. But my rivals stole the contracts for these designs and our men were put out of business. My rivals obtained effective claims which killed our business.

Mr. Lanham. What is the practical remedy?

The Chairman. We will come to that later.

Mr. Lanham. Mr. Martin says he is not coming back.

The Chairman. Are you afraid they will get rid of you?

Mr. Martin. I am not afraid of my life. I am ready to give up my life.

The Chairman. How much money do you have invested in your plant?

Mr. Martin. Up to 1925 many millions of dollars had been invested to develop my airplane inventions, as shown on this chart that I will pass to the chairman.

The Chairman. Do you object to having the chart incorporated into the record?

Mr. Martin. I have no objection. I have been robbed of money, of my reputation and patents. My airplanes have been destroyed by incendiary bombs, not by Germans, but worse than Germans, men living in this country who are double-crossing it and who are giving Japan the greatest incentive to make war against the United States.

Mr. (Charles V.) Truax. Do you refer to any of the Wall Street bankers and brokers who own and control possibly all of the air industry in the country?

Mr. Martin. There is a well-defined group of bankers and brokers who never devoted any time or money to aviation until they saw that the government was appropriating, in 1917, the sum of $640,000,000 for airplanes. They came in and by methods that even in a savage country would be regarded as dishonorable, they took over, by bribery and corruption, complete control of procurement in aviation of this government and proceeded to crush initiative from the outside and drove every independent company out of business.

The independents were ready to supply this government with thousands of fighting planes that had better performances than anything at the front. The monopoly, with finally $1,650,000,000 in its grip, had its own way. This whole conspiracy revolved around [Attorney General to Harding and Coolidge] Harry Daugherty and his gang ['The Ohio Gang,' corrupt political operators from Daugherty's Ohio Republican days.] and led to the murder of Jed Smith and probably to the poisoning of President Harding [Daugherty had been Harding's campaign manager and used the election to gain national prominence; but, despite poisoning rumors from all quarters, including even Harding's wife Florence, the 29th President died of natural causes, a heart-attack at age 58]. Bear in mind that this fraud involved several hundred million dollars, and anything could happen.

The Chairman. You have said that no one ever knew the real cause of the resignation of General Mitchell from the Army and that if the facts were known, the greatest tribute would be paid to him. Could you enlighten this committee about these facts?

Mr. Lanham. Unless in the opinion of General Mitchell, the question should be asked as to why he retired, should we ask Mr. Martin to testify about that? I think Mr. Martin would agree with that view.

Mr. Martin. I do not agree with it at all.

General Mitchell. (Present as a spectator). I do not care whether he states it.

Mr. Martin. It would not make any difference anyway.

The Chairman. Go ahead. Let us know it.

Mr. Martin. I was the consulting engineer at one time to the Air Service and I was directly in touch with it when General Mitchell met the difficulties that I will now outline to you. General Mitchell was in charge of operations of the Air Forces. That meant that when he ordered flights, they were made on his authority. And when he ordered that they be not made, they were not made. He was responsible for the operation of flying, which is a majority of all flying. There was one branch of the Air Service that he did not have anything to do with and unfortunately his recommendations about it were seldom taken. That was the engineering division. It was under the control of the colonel, who has been mentioned here and who headed the $1,650,000,000 monopoly. In 1912 that man was convicted and sentenced to jail, but he never served his sentence. In charge of the engineering division during the war he manipulated the money, gave our boys in France the "flaming coffins" and was at last recommended for prosecution by the Chief Justice of the United States. The bankers saved that man. He was the one General Mitchell was up against during the war. As I understand it, he is now the principal power in what we call the "Air Trust."

The Chairman. Go on about General Mitchell.

Mr. Martin. General Mitchell, as I say, had nothing to do with engineering. If a plane was defective, he could not correct that. If the structure of an airplane made it dangerous to use, he had no power or authority to correct that, but he had the responsibility over the lives of our splendid young men in the air service, aviators recruited from the ranks of the finest boys you can get anywhere, the most intelligent and the most courageous. These young men had to fly rotten, defective planes. General Mitchell had to give them the orders to fly in them. Such things as that would happen, and did happen, where a young man would come in and say, "You know, General, that the plane I have been ordered to fly in is not fit to make the flight." To which the General would say (whether he will admit it or not, and I know because I have been there), he would say, "Yes, I know, but that's what we have to fly in." Now, it is my opinion, Mr. Chairman, that General Mitchell could not stomach this condition much longer; sending his boys to their deaths in rattletrap planes. I think that is the major reason why he had to resign. He felt that his duty to the country superseded his fullest subordination, his supposed subordination, to the authorities in the Army, and that was something which the General took under consideration. I believe he sacrificed his career knowingly in order to try to correct a horrible situation and give our aviators decent airplanes to fly in.

If the nation knew the real facts, General Mitchell would be lauded and praised forever for this unselfish action and for a lot of other things that have never been disclosed. I have often urged the General to talk about these things and he has replied: "Well, Martin, what I have said already has branded me, through the Air Trust, as a radical or worse, and if I told the whole truth, nobody would listen to me at all!" That is one of the angles of this whole situation, Gentlemen. Recently our aviators demonstrated the deplorable and fatal policy of our Air Service by trying to carry the airmail. You laymen can understand if you use just a little of your own common sense, rather than listen to Air Trust propaganda, that if an airplane is not equipped properly, it does not make any difference how good your aviators are, and I will say now that the Army has the best of aviators.

But those men had such defective equipment that they could not even carry paper; namely, the mail! What in hell could they do in a war with such machines? Suppose they had to carry explosives over uncharted regions like the Pacific North West to reach Alaska and the Aleutian Islands. Think! Think, Gentlemen, for God's sake. The American people should wake up and support Congress to make a real, thorough and final investigation of these terrible charges, all of which are sustained. I can offer you a resume of the Lampert Committee records which show that all charges against the Air Trust were fully sustained but the country remains in the hands of a diabolical clique, a group of bankers and brokers who use the air funds of the people's government for their own profit and political influence. In return they do not give back to our government twenty-five cents of value on every dollar appropriated for airplane production. Here are some records to prove...

The Chairman. The meeting will stand adjourned subject to the call of the chairman.

The committee reconvened on February 20 when Martin was recalled and asked to continue his testimony, which was as follows from the record:

The Chairman. The committee has decided to hear more of your testimony, Mr. Martin. You may proceed.

Mr. Martin. Now, Gentlemen, if you would like to know where some of your money goes (in the aircraft industry) I think I can show you.

The Chairman. Go ahead.

Mr. Martin. As you are members of the Patent Committee, I think this will interest you. An Englishman, by the name of Handley-Page, came to this country with an application for a certain patent which, on an airplane, is called the "slotted wing." He filed that patent, secured it to be issued, sold it to the government for $1,000,000, collected $125,000 of it and left the country, all within a period of ninety days. That is what I call swift movement, considering my own experiences, as an American, with the Patent Office of our government.

It happens that this Handley-Page patent, in-so-far as the $1,000,000 contract was concerned, was a device which has never been used. There is no dispute about it. It has never been used on one plane in the United States.

The Chairman. You mean that the patent Mr. Page received from the Patent Office, for which the government paid him $1,000,000 has never been used on any airplane?

Mr. Martin. Not quite that way. He received $125,000 on account but he was not paid $1,000,000. I brought the matter to the attention of a Congressional Committee, which asked Mr. Wilbur, then the Secretary of the Navy, to appear. He said he had stopped further payments, but while the Attorney General was trying to get the money back Handley-Page had received $250,000 before this flow of money was stopped. It was subsequently disclosed in England that Handley-Page had obtained the idea for the "slotted wing" from a German prisoner of war. I was vitally interested in the matter, as I had a basic patent on the same device filed four years before Handley-Page appeared in this country. I had an adjudication of the Patent Office that my invention was prior.

The Chairman. How could that patent have been granted to Mr. Page by the Patent Office when you had priority rights four years before?

Mr. Martin. Because Handley-Page's patent was what we call an improvement patent, a specific application on my basic patent, but before I received my patent, I had to satisfy the Commissioner that I was the prior inventor. I satisfied him and he issued my patent but since then I have been unable to get even a small sum for my basic patent, whereas the gentlemen of the Air Trust, as Handley-Page did, can get those types of contracts.

The Chairman. Your patent was infringed upon?

Mr. Martin. Yes. My basic patent was not issued to me until after the Handley-Page contract was signed.

The Chairman. Did Handley-Page keep the money?

Mr. Martin. Yes. I would have had to prove within one year after Handley-Page got his license that he was not the owner of the invention. By the time the Patent Office found out that I was the original inventor, it was too late. Page kept all the money.

The Chairman. What became of all those planes that were made during the war and never got to France? I understand that General Mitchell received only 196 of them.

Mr. Martin. Some of them were destroyed, deliberately burned, others were suppressed in various ways, while independent companies, which could have made first class fighting machines, were put out of business by the Trust.

Mr. (J. Burrwood) Daly. How many lives were lost during experiments with these defective planes?

Mr. Martin. The lives lost in experimenting with those machines far exceeded the number of American aviators lost in the war. My records show that we lost ten boys a day for a long period of time, due wholly to inferior ships.

The Chairman. Why are these planes referred to as "flaming coffins"?

Mr. Martin. Because they were built so that the gasoline tanks were directly behind the pilot. Even fire-proofing of the tanks had been discarded. It would not have mattered much anyhow as the Germans soon discovered where the large tanks were located and shot incendiary darts into them. The planes burst into flames, burning the pilots alive in midair. The whole Air Force called them "flaming coffins."

The Chairman. Were you asked to build these planes at the time?

Mr. Martin. When the Air Trust was originally conceived, I was invited to attend one of its conferences. I was assured that it would have $10,000,000 in the bank for me, so that I could start operations. That was quite a lot of money for a struggling man. I told the Colonel who headed the combination: "I will be glad indeed to make my services available to the government and I will bring my experts to Ohio immediately to do the inside work."

I added that I had valuable designs prepared and ready, but the organizers said: "You can forget all about that because we are going to make the De Haviland 4." I said I would not be a party to any such arrangements; I would not be a party in the building of the

DH4 because I knew what it was, in comparison with the other machines at the front. The DH4 had been copied from an old type of British machine, was already obsolescent and I knew that by the time we had built them, they would have been obsolete.

That is what happened. That is why they were no good in the war. I told the combination our aviators would be at the mercy of the enemy in such a machine. I turned the proposition down and then my troubles started.

The Chairman. Do you know of any independent inventor or any independent agency that has perfected any invention capable of passing by the monopoly?

Mr. Martin. Whenever there was an official report showing actual flight superiority it disappeared in the government offices. Photographs were destroyed. The Lampert Investigating Committee discovered that fact. I know of an American inventor who perfected a device to completely control that most dangerous feature of stability, the lateral control. The device was tested on a government Army plane and flew so successfully that the old ailerons were completely taken off the ship and the pilot flew it across the country without any controls available, through gusty winds and with great ease.

All the official reports of this accomplishment were destroyed in the War Department. The inventor then went to England and flew this device on a British airplane so that three men in the machine, the observer, a motion picture man and the pilot, got out on the wings of the plane and flew over the North Sea with no one inside at the controls.

The Chairman. As a well-known aircraft pioneer and inventor were you asked to give your views before the Dwight Morrow Board?

Mr. Martin. No.

Mr. Daly. Are you prevented from getting redress from the Air Trust?

Mr. Martin. Yes. Under the Act of July 1, 1918, a patent owned by an inventor can be "legally" stolen by the monopoly. The act prevents the inventor from protecting his patent. This is known as the "save harmless" clause in government contracts with the Trust.

Mr. Lucas. I have heard your testimony and General Mitchell's and it certainly is sensational. You believe every effort should be made to break up the Air Trust?

Mr. Martin. I solemnly believe that unless, in some way or other, you can eradicate the Air Trust, we will have to fight a very disastrous war with Japan. In other words, Japan knows that we cannot get decent aircraft as long as we are the victims of this internal corruption, and unless we can get this matter before the public and arouse national sentiment we will be lost.

The Chairman. Do the Japanese have planes that can go more than 2,500 miles?

Mr. Martin. Yes, with a weight of bombs, in some cases exceeding 6,000 pounds and a speed of considerably more than 200 miles an hour.

The Chairman. Do we have in the Army or the Navy or the Air Corps one machine that can do that?

Mr. Martin. No.

The Chairman. In spite of the fact that we have spent during the last war $1,650,000,000 for aircraft development and did not have a ship that could go up, and since that time to the present, a period of seventeen years, have spent more than $1,400,000,000 in aeronautical development, and not one machine that can compare with those of the Italian flyers recently here?

Mr. Martin. That is correct. I have records here to show that the War Department turned down bombers in 1925 that could make 200 miles an hour. The Lampert Committee reported at that time: "In the event that it is approximately 3,000 miles across the Atlantic, if these planes of Martin's could start from England, they could carry 2,000 pounds of bombs and bomb New York and intern in Canada."

The Chairman. If that is true, is it not then a matter of fact that Japanese planes could fly over to the Aleutian Islands in four or five hours, and since we have no fortifications whatsoever, either for supplementing the Navy or the Army there, the Japanese could start from the Aleutians and in five or six hours bombard California, or Oregon or the State of Washington and return, at the height of 35,000 feet in the air where no one could see them?

Mr. Martin. That could be done right now, and we could do nothing about it.

Mr. Daly. If the Japanese get to Alaska, is it probable that they could bombard any city on the Western seaboard, and we would be powerless?

Mr. Martin. I think they could make a base that would be perfectly safe for them on the Aleutian Islands. I believe it is all part of their plans. I am familiar with that territory because I have made twelve trips to Japan as a navigator and I know it is entirely possible for the Japanese to capture a base in the Aleutians and from that base to operate to the West Coast cities. Their planes could then fly east and bomb the Eastern cities.

The Chairman. Using the Aleutians as a base could not the Japanese operate to destroy the Panama Canal?

Mr. Martin. I understand they have made easier provisions for that project. They have secured concessions in the Central American States and from there they are prepared to fly to the Canal. It does not take a big bomb to create a slide on the sides of the Canal.

Recalled again by the Committee on Patents on February 28, the inventor continued his testimony, part of which follows:

Mr. Martin. I have come into possession of verified information which may interest your committee. The biggest aircraft company in this country during the last war was controlled by Japan, Germany's fiscal agent here. A man, who was assistant manager of this company, and whose name I will give you for the record, is ready to testify that the company was not only owned by the Japanese but that seventy-eight carloads of airplanes that were bought and paid for by our taxpayers' money were shipped to Japan under the label "Household Furniture."

The Chairman. We will discuss that privately.

Mr. Lanham. You believe this country is falling behind in modern engines of defense because its inventive genius is being suppressed by the Air Trust?

Mr. Martin. Yes. Japan and other nations are ahead of us because our inventors are persecuted and driven out of the country. Count Zeppelin had his start in this country and then perfected dirigibles. The German submarine that made war a menace for us was invented by an American who was offered no encouragement by the Army and Navy. I speak of Simon Lake, because he had processes that were finally sold to Germany. He was not able to get his own country to take his device. After I had invented the retractable chassis for airplanes, I was told by the Secretary of the Navy and the Secretary of War over their own signatures, to take my invention to any country in the world, to do anything I wanted with it. Of course, those gentlemen did not know what they were doing; they were being guided by this Aircraft Trust. Officers of the Air Corps actually refer inventors to the Trust, to be turned down. All this is verified by letters available to you.

The Chairman. I have some very important work to do, Mr. Martin. Suppose we give you some morning next week to finish your testimony. Next week Thursday. The committee will stand adjourned.

Martin, having waited until March 7, compelled to defray his own expenses in Washington over a week's period, was called for the last time to deliver his concluding testimony, part of which follows:

The Chairman. Mr. Martin, you have made the most serious charges that this committee has heard during the ten years I have been a member of it. We want you now to summarize completely the accusations against the monopoly in order that the committee may take one action or the other.

Mr. Martin proceeded patiently to read his own digest of all the facts, which filled twenty-seven pages of his own testimony when it was sent to the government printing house. These facts in increasing numbers had for eighteen years been available in the many volumes of records of aircraft investigations stored away in Congressional vaults, and about which nothing had been done.

The Chairman (Sitting with the Committee after listening to the inventor for five hours). Is it your theory that these same corrupt forces that prevailed during the Republican administration still exist under the Democratic Administration?

Mr. Martin. The same thing is going on in full swing in the procurement divisions of the Army and Navy. I am happy to say there has been some reform in the Department of Commerce.

The Chairman. The reason I am interested in your testimony is that I have found facts to convince me that a war is coming. I am certain we will have to defend ourselves from Japan.

Mr. Kramer. Last August (in 1934) as chairman of the Sub-committee on un-American Activities, I was informed in Los Angeles that Japanese fishing boats are so arranged to carry torpedoes and mines from a distance of 3,000 miles at sea. These fishing boats are equipped with long distance and very powerful radio equipment. This seems entirely unnecessary in a fishing boat. Plans were introduced before our committee by the firm which built these ships to show that these boats, in the middle of the sea, can be equipped within an hour with mines and torpedoes. Japan has prepared them in this way. We all agreed that it was worth looking into.

Mr. Martin. We could make it practically impossible to have war with Japan by removing dishonest control from the procurement divisions of the Army and Navy. Japan is in a fortunate position. She used to have to support her espionage out of her own funds. Now the aircraft monopoly is doing that for her at our taxpayers' expenses.

The Chairman. Is Japan aware of all the patents we have and does the monopoly sell Japan bombing planes that we ought to have and which could be furnished to us?

Mr. Martin. Just as fast as we independent inventors submit data to the Air Corps of the Navy, it is transmitted to the Air Trust with which our government does business. Japan gets her information directly as a business proposition. You will recall the "Household Furniture" shipments I have described to you.

The Chairman. In other words, our taxpayers are paying for the national defense of Japan?

Mr. Martin. They certainly are.

Mr. (Matthew A.) Dunn. According to this testimony, the big fellows in the United States are looked up to, today, while they point fingers at other men, struggling for humanity's sake, and who are called communists and thrown into jail. And yet the finger pointers are the biggest thieves in the world.

Mr. Lucas. Does the witness believe that our Western coast is in danger of attack from Japan?

Mr. Martin. I flew in Alaska eight years before anyone else ever flew there. That is the place to watch first. The Japanese are not worried about our resources. What do they care for our resources while they know that inside the United States corruption has ruined every airplane program that has been attempted in eighteen years?

Mr. Kramer. Our American fisheries and canneries in Alaska employ Japanese mostly. I have been looking things over up there.

The Chairman. When were those train-loads of planes shipped to Japan as "Furniture"?

Mr. Martin. That was near the close of the last war. The shipment consisted of large bombing airplanes.

Mr. Dunn. How many independent aircraft corporations are there in the United States?

Mr. Martin. There are none now. I am probably the last one of the independents to go to complete starvation. I am on the verge of starvation now. My factory has had no work for years although foreign governments in their highest laboratories certify that my designs held world's records for efficiency. This has all been admitted as sworn testimony before the Lampert Committee.

The Chairman. Most of these independent inventors whose patents were stolen died in poverty?

Mr. Martin. They died in poverty: Jannen, Farber and many others including Herring. Two years after Herring's death the Court of Appeals of the State of New York held that he had been deprived of his patents and his stock interest. Nearly all the old inventors I brought before the Lampert Investigation Committee in 1925 died in poverty.

Mr. Lucas. How many inventions were stolen from you?

Mr. Martin. Forty-seven, altogether; twenty-two on all the modern airplanes. The use of eight of my inventions is indispensable in getting a license to fly.

Mr. (Ralph E.) Church. Why do you not press your claims further?

The Chairman. He doesn't have any money.

Mr. Martin. I have been pressing my claims in the Court of Appeals for ten years to bring my matters to trial. I am reduced to poverty. I have no money to pay witnesses. The court reporter's bill to me in one case this year was $800.

The Chairman. How long will it take you to finish this testimony?

Mr. Martin. I'm about finished, Mr. Chairman.

Mr. Church. Could Colonel Lindbergh help us with this investigation?

Mr. Martin. I think if Colonel Lindbergh appeared before this Committee, it would be on behalf of the Air Trust which is his present employer.

Mr. Lucas. You have testified that your product was destroyed by your competitors.

Mr. Martin. Yes. I had a plane actually built in 1926 that had all the characteristics and mileage required to take a crew across the Atlantic. It was destroyed by incendiary darts shot into it by my aircraft competitors' agents within the Army Air Service.

The Chairman. Have you anything further to add?

Mr. Martin. I will close with one request. Remember the sacrifices of my friend, General Billy Mitchell.

16 - WINGS OF THE MORNING

NEWSPAPER EDITORS SEARCHING THE country for front page sensations had become tired of Billy Mitchell's predictions when the final hearings of the investigation of the aircraft patent-pool were launched in New York. Although military experts talked frankly of approaching war, late in 1935, headline craftsmen considered the air crusader as out of fashion.

His warning messages were flung into the wicker baskets which fringe the copy desks. LaGuardia, "little Mayor of the Big City" was campaigning to abate the noise rising from large populations and had started by chasing organ-grinders out of town.

Not much later, as time goes, he was to plead for the loudest air raid sirens that could be turned out to scream at 7,000,000 people. To the citizen who supports out of his own pocket the arms of defense, the technicalities of the patent-probe may have been too boring to absorb. People begin to understand these complicated affairs when bombs rain about them and blast their houses to matchsticks while victims cower in air shelters with their helpless families.

The picture becomes clearer when one reads that brave General Claire L. Chennault, armed with a few obsolescent P-40's for his American Flying Tigers in China has to fight an enemy flaunting an overwhelming number of the best American bombers and pursuit planes, all built in Japan under United States license and supervised during their construction by highly paid experts of an American monopoly. It had become an open secret that Mitchell dominated the inquiry launched to break up the aircraft combination. It may be revealed now that he was the inquiry's directing force though he worked incessantly under the growing handicap of a heart ailment. He was not only concerned with the attack on patent-pooling but with his own rehabilitation and with the circumvention of an impressive circle of enemies determined to prolong his inactivity.

He used his friend, the newspaperman, now an investigator to help him in his plans, and sent him here and there from one part of the country to another, wherever it appeared that his presence could be of use. Mitchell had prevailed upon Representative Sirovich, the chairman of the Investigating Committee to obtain an appropriation for the collection of evidence which finally amounted to $25,000, a sum which the General said was merely a "drop in the bucket" for such work.

The crusader expressed his impatience with Sirovich, who was struggling daily under a deluge of new legislation of his own creation: A campaign to revise the copyright act to protect "Tin Pan Alley;" a measure for new safeguards for passenger ships; a bill to create a Department of Science, Art and Literature in the government with a Secretary of Fine Arts in the Cabinet.

The Congressman was trying to accomplish a task impossible for any one man. He was purposeful in his actions and well-meaning, a kindly bachelor who visited his mother's grave regularly. War being horrifying to him, airplanes represented in his mind a symbol of death and destruction. He surrounded himself with long-haired poets and playwrights interested in his art legislation and the new humanism. Forced to fight his way through a regiment of these geniuses one day, to see Sirovich, the General remarked dryly to his friend, "Christ! Art may be a good thing for the country, but if we don't get any planes, we won't have any art."

Among the records the General had turned over to Chairman Sirovich to be revealed at the hearings was a significant report prepared by Senator Ernest Lundeen who believed navies were outdated. He had presented a bill to create a government bureau to regulate commercial navigation of the air.

He was killed with twenty other passengers in an airplane crash which, ironically, he had described as a type of accident most easily avoidable. One of the Senator's disclosures which Mitchell verified threw a significant light on the ease with which foreign powers obtained American-made weapons, even though the State Department stepped in to prevent such transactions. In 1935, attaches of Soviet Russia approached American manufacturers of tanks and bombing planes with an order involving several millions of dollars. The American firms were enthusiastic, but a few days later became lukewarm. The Russians offered to place the business on a cash basis but were turned down. The State Department had stipulated that American tanks and planes could not be sold to Russia, while, in the meantime, Japan was being plentifully supplied with airplanes from the United States. Nevertheless, Russia obtained both tanks and planes. She bought them in England and Germany, and they were identical with those which were to have been ordered in the United States.

American manufacturers, seeing immense contracts slipping through their fingers, sold the patents which they controlled to British Vickers and German Junkers and in return received a ten percent commission on the order. Russia was satisfied and, incidentally, Germany became acquainted with the detailed plans of some of our most up-to-date weapons, including those going to Moscow.

The General's activities behind the Patent Committee were of such common repute in Army and industrial aircraft circles that he was fairly certain he was being "shadowed" by agents, about whom he had warned his investigative assistant. Washington reporters again nibbled at the rumors that the former Air Chief would be made "Aviation Czar" of the Nation. For some reason, this apparently had an irritating effect on General Hugh S. Johnson, then writing a daily column which he produced after the manner of an artilleryman behind a six-pounder. He turned his editorial cannon on Mitchell, who soon was satisfied that the attack had been instigated by the "brass heads" of the War Department.

Reflecting a hostility that reached back at least fifteen years, "Old Iron Pants" raked up the aircraft-seacraft controversy to tell his readers the air crusader had accomplished nothing. Mitchell read these fulminations with curling lips.

"The Old Bomber!" he chuckled, "he's nose heavy!"

There could not have been a better example than Johnson's broadsides to depict the attitude of the old-style Army men, then in the saddle, toward Mitchell's cause. The opposition of the War Department to his ideas was to continue long after his death, for ridicule and contempt were to be heaped even upon his grave.

Six years after Billy Mitchell had passed on, his predictions vindicated, "Old Iron Pants," was still embalming in print the views of the General Staff, ignoring the new instrument which had thrown into the discard all the old conceptions of warfare.

"I knew Billy Mitchell from youth," Johnson wrote. "I served with him frequently. He was an air enthusiast with the showmanship of P. T. Barnum. Before the World War a cavalryman was considered no good unless he believed as a religion that cavalry could lick double its weight in any other arm by a mounted charge. Just about that time the artillery was getting cocky. To hear the gunners, talk, new methods of fire control had obsoleted everything on any battlefield. For several recent years the enthusiasms of aviators has insisted on the complete futility of anything that doesn't fly.

"Billy Mitchell was given every reasonable privilege to prove his thesis, even to being permitted to try to sink, from the air, several million dollars' worth of actual battleship. It was finally done, but under no reasonable conditions of actual warfare. When he tested under those conditions he failed. Bombing raids on naval bases have been purely experimental. On all the proved evidence yet, all have flopped. What the mass suicide raid may do remains to be seen. But nothing has happened yet to disturb the bones of Billy Mitchell."

General Johnson's conclusions were based on the same stupefying logic which was to prompt General MacArthur, with both feet planted solidly in the Philippines, (before Pearl Harbor) to say to the magazine writer, Edgar Snow:

"Japan will never attack us here as long as our main fleet is in the Pacific."

But Mitchell was not to read of what happened to Bataan or to the airplane hangars laid out in serried rows at Hawaii.

One evening in December of 1935, when the aircraft hearings were being held at the Fifth Avenue Hotel in New York City, Jimmy Martin, the former mariner and pioneer airplane inventor, burst into the suite where Mitchell and the investigator were scrutinizing a new batch of evidence, much of which had to do with the sale of American airplanes to Japan.

"Let's take a ride down to the docks, General," the old inventor suggested. "I've been prowling around there. You may be interested to see what I saw. It isn't anything new but, right under your eyes, it hammers the facts home."

As Martin had said, it was an old waterfront story, the subject of occasional jokes in the Broadway wise-cracking columns and the nightclubs. On the docks or trimming ship were little slant-eyed, sweating men, bared to the waist, unmindful of the winter wind, working like ants around hills of junk, some running nimbly on little legs down gangplanks into the shadows directing American loaders carrying baskets heaped with rusty ore, nails, spikes, pipe, cast off stoves, freight-car wheels, broken kettles, even horseshoes brought across the country, perhaps from abandoned farms.

Under the bluish glare of arc lights, derricks incessantly swung heavier parts of the metal; girders, long spans of rails from torn-down elevated railroads, all to be flung as though no time was to spare, into the holds of grimy, battered freighters flying the familiar white flag with the bright red ball.

"The one on the end is filled up," Martin shouted through the din.

"She's leaving tonight. I talked to her captain today. Let's have a final look at her."

A black-hulled freighter abreast of the dock, its belly full, poured jets of acrid, farewell smoke over its crew, feverish with homeward-bound preparations.

"Captain Kushuda!" Martin bawled out in a fog-horn voice, his hand at his mouth. "Captain Kushuda!"

A little leathery man popped out on the lighted deck in a soiled white uniform, adjusting his cap.

"Oh, yes!" he recognized Martin. "Come say goodbye?"

"All loaded up?" Martin asked.

"Yes," Captain Kushuda grinned. "Big load this time. Maybe last time. I don't know."

"All scrap iron?" Martin persisted.

"Yes, scrap iron for Japan."

"When do you go through the Panama Canal?"

"Maybe Friday. Slow trip this time. Too heavy!"

The captain waved his hand to someone in the cabin, a signal for the steam whistle which enveloped the watchers with long, cold, shrill wails of sound. Another load of bullets for Japan.

"That'll go on," Martin said, "until they're ready to shoot it back at us."

Mitchell cast over his shoulder a last grim look at the freighter. "Scrap iron," he spat. "Well named! We're selling 'em everything we've got!"

To be close to the General during the last year of his life was to understand the vast influence he spread constantly like giant wings over the Army Air Service. He referred to its members as "my boys." He had brought the best of them up. They were saturated with his doctrines. They all believed a unified command of Air would come and prayed for it. Some of them, who, in their zeal had testified in the General's behalf ten years before at his court-martial had been cruelly penalized. "Happy" Arnold, who, during his Chief's trial, had, with brave defiance, protested the use of the "flaming coffins" and warned the court of America's lack of air power had been exiled to the "sticks," as Mitchell had been after his own demotion.

Arnold, like a boy sent to a truants' school, was compelled to start from the bottom of the service after his testimony. By persistence and ability, he had worked up the ladder again from Fort Riley, Kansas. He had not forgotten a word Mitchell had taught him. He kept his mouth shut but wrote recommendations regularly.

The General's eyes glittered with pride when he read, during a breathing spell in the investigation, a report of an air survey of Alaska, accomplished in an able flight led by his pupil "Happy" Arnold, who won the Mackay Trophy for the second time as a result.

The Army had finally decided to take a strategic look at Alaska, prodded into the decision by Arnold who remembered Mitchell's warning about "the top of the world," and his former chief's markings on the globe back in those days at "Boxwood."

The General Staff had finally decided to recognize the strategic importance of the Territory after fishing out, somewhat belatedly, the old recommendation Mitchell had written on the air survey, fifteen years ago.

"'Hap' Arnold is coming along," the General commented, with the glow of Mr. Chips reviewing the achievements of his youngsters. "He's a Brigadier General now, the rank I once had. He'll lead the Air Corps. I don't think he's fifty yet, but he grew up with airplanes. He has all the essentials of leadership. And he knows the importance of Alaska. That's the jumping off place to smash Japan. If we wait to fight her in the Philippines, it'll take us five years to lick her. But 'Hap' Arnold knows the story. I've told it to him often enough."

As the investigation progressed, Mitchell, working tirelessly into the night to sift the evidence and prepare the questions which were shot at the leaders of the aircraft monopoly on the witness stand, began to show unmistakable signs of a grave illness. His keen face had become drawn, obviously twisted with pain from the region of his heart.

His ailment, at times, must have caused him excruciating agony, and Sirovich, a physician, who, incidentally, suffered from the same disease, gave the General restoratives to use when the attacks came on. The investigator now and again had to watch the crusader recover from paroxysms and then apply himself once more to his papers with a shake of the head as though defying a persistent sense of impending death.

On the last evening that the General dropped into "Little Venice," he had just returned from Washington where he had seen the President. He was noncommittal about the conference, but made a remark about his visit which carried some significance to his friends at the table.

"The President's desk," he said, "is covered with all sorts of gimcracks, gifts of every variety from his friends—mostly little trinkets. While I was talking to him, I noticed all kinds of miniatures of things you see on boats: ships' clocks, steering wheels, life preservers—well, things that reflect a man's love of the sea. I wish I could have seen an airplane model in that collection."

The General ordered a bourbon highball and drank it slowly, looking at his glass after each slight swallow as at some forbidden enjoyment, partaken for the last time and to be prolonged.

He seemed haggard and worn, but somehow, he had an air about him, something that could not be beaten by life. He was disturbed by surprising developments which affected the investigation. In his fight for reinstatement he had been anxious to enlist the services of Senator Huey Long who had promised his support to Mitchell, but who had just been assassinated at Baton Rouge.

A subpoena had been prepared to be served upon Colonel Lindbergh to appear at the hearings, but while the "Lone Eagle" was being sought he had suddenly left for Europe with his family under circumstances which The New York Times in its exclusive report characterized as "mysterious."

Mitchell's opinions on Lindbergh and the aircraft monopoly ramifications were contained in a letter which he wrote to the patent pool investigator, four months before the flyer left for Europe, and which follows in part:

BOXWOOD MIDDLEBURG, VA
August 1, 1935
My dear Gauvreau:
I have been in Dr. Sirovich's office at the beginning of each week and he has explained to me what is going on. I know that you are making good progress.

However, I want to impress on you that the pool of patents, while it has a great many interesting side issues which bear on it and particularly on the monopoly angle of it, was started in the summer of 1917. The name of its leading spirit at that time is on official record.

He was succeeded by another individual also of official record who made a horrible show of things. The third and present successor, the active head of these interests is the one that directs the lobbying activities here (in Washington) and a great deal of the disposal of the equipment to foreign countries, including Japan, by whom he has been decorated with the Order of the Rising Sun.

I think it is very necessary to find out the financial background of the company we discussed. While there is a mass of data on other companies brought out before the Black Committee, the company I refer to escaped the greater part of this investigation. It was very clever in avoiding it also. When the time comes to inspect the papers of this company, great care will have to be taken that it is done without its knowledge and suddenly, otherwise it will be very adept at covering up and destroying incriminating matter.

As to Lindbergh, he is a commercial flyer. His motive is principally profit. He was a barnstormer and airmail pilot before his flight to Europe. This flight was well prepared and executed. Of course, there was a certain element of luck in it. His deportment after it and the way everything was handled gave him remarkable prominence in this country and over the world.

At first, the Air Trust didn't know what to make of it. Some articles appeared attempting to belittle his flight, notably one by Grover Loening, but it was too good a show to pass unnoticed. Therefore, they decided to use him, and immediately upon his return they made overtures to him. He has been used by them to attract capital to their ventures, and behind which a good deal of this speculation has taken place in aviation stocks. He used a certain engine in his transatlantic flight and a great point was made of this also. Lindbergh's influence has been used by these interests against a united Air Service. He is advised largely by an Admiral connected with construction and repair for the Navy. . . .

Since the findings of the Morrow Board were put into effect, our aviation has sunk lower and lower... Lindbergh is tied in with that group very effectively.

You must realize that this is also a clever group and that they have ramifications here, particularly in the Navy.

It should not be hard for you to establish how they have made use of Lindbergh for the purpose of carrying out their various designs. You will notice that this group all along the line have not attempted to support any definite concrete policy except to make money for themselves, under any and all conditions.

The people they have picked up and made much of are what might be termed "stunt artists", such as Amelia Earhart, a commercial flyer, Frank Hawks, Roscoe Turner and others. These people, while excellent pilots, particularly Miss Earhart, are very much in the nature of theatrical performers as far as their influence on the development of aircraft is concerned. This includes Lindbergh.

As to R. H. Fleet, he came from the Pacific Coast, he and his father both being prominent in their section, Washington State, I think. He came into the service during the War and did well in this country, being finally put in charge of contracts, payments and a great deal of the procurement, which he did very well and very honestly. When the Air Service was reorganized and he was to be given only a minor position, he decided to resign, went back to civil life and organized one of the best airplane companies in this country.

He beat the other crowd at their own game. He consistently held out from the Air Trust. They sued him for infringement of patents on eleven counts. He decided to fight them. Eight of the infringements charged, he decided, did not amount to anything but three might.

At this period, he had a very bad crash which nearly killed him and while he was ill, his directors decided to join the monopoly. In his testimony before the House Military Committee, Fleet stated that "the pool of patents was a decided detriment to the improvement of aircraft in this country", or words to that effect.

Fleet has furnished good equipment to the government, as it goes. In one instance a contract was made with him in which it was determined afterward that he had made excessive profits, so he sold the government a number of aircraft, I think it was ten, for $1, to make up the excess money which he received.

Fleet continues to receive large contracts from the government. It would be a good thing for you to have a talk with him. He will talk very straight from the shoulder with you. He is quite different from the crowd around the man decorated by Japan.

I hope that you will not be carried away too far by side issues before you get at the main proposition. I think the general layout that Dr. Sirovich *explained to me is excellent. I hope this answers your questions. If not, let me know and I will write you further.*

Sincerely,

Wm. Mitchell

"The newspapers," the General said, "are not interested in the patent-pool disclosures because they see nothing dramatic in them. But the pool, as it affects the public interest, that is, the defense of the country, is a dangerous industrial conception. The individual acquiring ownership of many patents has one of two objects in view. Either he seeks to gain control of the industry to which the patents relate and thus wipe out competition, or he wants to suppress such patents as he believes would be detrimental to him in their exploitation. The public suffers in either case and the patent laws are violated. There you have our aviation situation in a nutshell. We refuse to realize what this means to the country. We're like so many hitchhikers thumbing a ride on the road to hell."

The General was concerned about the strategy of tanks to be used in co-operation with airplanes. He had received information that a report submitted by Colonel J. K. Parsons to the War Department, almost six years before, recommending the organization of six divisions of 486 tanks each, had been pigeonholed.

"Tanks, like planes," Mitchell said, "are something new. The two things go together, and they'll win the next war. In the meantime, our 'brass heads' are still fighting the motorization of their cavalry divisions. They'll never get 'Squads right!' out of their heads. I hope the poor damned fools escape the bombs on their horses."

Mitchell saw all too clearly the destructive events which engulfed the world less than four years after his last prophecies. He was the forgotten man of the Army. In the deadly parallel of experience, he might have been compared with General Charles de Gaulle who as a Colonel in France, while Mitchell's life was ebbing out, urged the mechanization of the French Army and the formation of the very Panzer divisions which were used later by Hitler to bring France to her knees.

For his pains, de Gaulle, who also had begged for a vitalizing increase in the French Air Force, was dismissed from the General Staff. Only until then was the pigeonholed report of Colonel Parsons dusted off by our War Department which found itself with just one mechanized tank brigade and was amazed to discover that the devastating Panzer divisions of the Germany Army followed the Parsons plan.

As the final month of 1935 wore on Mitchell's last spark of hope of attracting public attention to the aviation situation was kindled by an eight-column headline in the New York Herald Tribune announcing that seventy-four per cent of a poll taken by Dr. George Gallup demanded an immediate increase in the United States Air Forces. America was already seeing visions of the Second World War and by an overwhelming majority favored greater appropriations for the Air arm.

Said the Gallup article: "'It's the Air Force, not the Navy anymore, that's our first line of defense,' thus writes an American whose beliefs are shared by millions like him."

The General was tremendously impressed, and his spirits rose as he studied the poll's figures. "If Washington wants to lead," he remarked wryly, "it should find out which way the people are running and then run ahead of them. Our so-called leaders may pay an awful price someday if the people discover they have been misled."

The only important editor who had anything to say about airplanes during Mitchell's last three months on earth was Arthur Brisbane, who in his old age expressed growing concern about the possibility of the bombing of his New York real estate. Addressing his 30,000,000 readers, he wrote crisply:

"A big United States Navy plane flew two thousand miles from Norfolk to the Canal. Fine. Now multiply the size of the plane by two, multiply the length of the hop by three and add fifteen hundred miles and you equal Russia's record. In the air we are fifth class. Even a gorilla could figure this out."

Chairman Sirovich had decided to put General Mitchell on the witness stand once again in an effort to stir public interest in the hearings. Although the subject had been dry from the standpoint of exciting news it had developed evidence of vast significance to the nation. It had been established that American aircraft industries were selling the best weapons they could make to Germany and Japan. The Emperor of Japan had expressed his pleasure to at least one aircraft leader by decorating him with the Order of the Rising Sun. Industrial chiefs countered with the claim that their companies could not possibly maintain themselves by limiting their orders to the government.

Stockholders were complaining about dividends; salaries amounting, in some cases, to $200,000 a year had to be paid to general managers who were forced to turn to foreign markets to sell their war goods. The fact that our own bombers were already obsolete and that American fighter planes had two guns less than the most up-to-date German and Japanese models did not interest the businessmen. Their alibi was that they were ready to sell to anybody, including the War Department, if more modern equipment was desired. There was no law to stop it.

Mitchell braced himself for a final emphatic plea to the nation to realize that the truth of the ominous situation could hardly be expected to be found in the explanations of the soulless profit-seeking Air Trust.

In a last burst of energy which drained his strength, he exposed the collusion and financial influences which dominated the Army Service's policy in awarding airplane contracts to the favored agents of the monopoly in the government procurement divisions.

He disclosed that not one single American aircraft unit then in use was fit for war purposes, while conniving foreign powers were outclassing America in the air.

He charged and proposed to prove that of the three billion dollars spent on aircraft in the United States during and since the first World War, nothing had been contributed to the safety of the Nation; nothing to the progress of aviation.

Patiently and painfully he explained why the patent-pool was a menace to the welfare of the country. Then, as he stepped slowly from the stand, his hand went to his heart with a convulsive movement.

Later, stretched out on a bed, Mitchell, breathing in gasps, asked for the newspapers. When he was propped up against the pillows, he turned the pages with trembling fingers and dropped the copies on the floor. Bits of his testimony were tucked away in obscure columns under small headings lost among great blocks of advertising of latest model automobiles and balloon tires.

One paper had squeezed an item under a small story of his testimony, and he read it with a shake of the head and a smile almost wistful, before handing the paper to the investigator.

"Here," the General said weakly, "you like irony. Read it out loud."

It was a bit of news from France entitled "Gay Gloves" and the investigator's voice faltered as he read:

"'Colored gloves are popular in Paris. Long turquoise blue suede gloves are worn with a black and white evening gown. On the boulevards in the afternoon your correspondent has noted long violet gloves with small, chic violet hats.'

"Paris," the General said tenderly, "Paris, after Noyon, Fère-en-Tardenois, St. Mihiel. I hope she may always wear her colored gloves."

He seemed to fall asleep after Sirovich had given him a sedative. The crusader at last had thundered his final message to the people, but the people were interested in other things. Martin was arranging his pillow.

"Is it pretty bad, Doctor?" Martin asked, drying his eyes with a red bandanna handkerchief.

"I know how bad it is!" The words came from Mitchell's bed.

"But," he said, "remember, someone will have to keep fighting. If we don't know those things which are of use and necessity for us to know we will be done for. Voluntary ignorance is criminal. We are neglecting an evil we refuse to learn how to prevent. I've been court-martialed for saying so. Generals may die in bed, but their battle plans remain."

He continued to talk slowly.

"Those who are supposed to protect us don't even know that anti-aircraft gunners can be trained only by actual fighting experience. We don't know that it takes 30,000 parts to make a bomber. When this thing breaks, we'll find out that the continuous operation of one big first-line plane requires up to 100 men on the ground and in the air. Five thousand planes will need 500,000 officers and men. But we'll need 100,000 planes; and more. Think of the number of men! And we're doing nothing about it."

"What's the matter with the people, anyhow!" Martin burst out.

"The people are all right," the General retorted. "Don't worry about them. They're ahead of those supposed to lead them. I'll never forget I got my permission to bomb the Ostfriesland from the people; from their elected representatives. They wanted to know if a battleship could be sunk from the air. The Army and Navy didn't want to know. Never underestimate the native common sense of the American people."

Mitchell returned to Boxwood in an attempt to recapture the strength which his crusade had drained from him. At the end of January 1936, he had to be removed to Doctors Hospital in New York. While he was climbing into his deathbed the House Military Affairs Committee killed a bill which would have retired him as a colonel with a government pittance.

When he died, his personal estate amounted to $5,765.

Meanwhile, he lay against his pillow, his records, papers and plans in his lap, his keen eyes upon the hospital window, straining to catch a glimpse of the airplanes which he heard far overhead. For days, the sky remained blue behind white, with racing winter clouds. Every day from his bed he watched them while the nurse counted his fading pulse, and every day at sunset, the westward gold touched his brave unconquered brow.

The investigator, who was not inclined to be superstitious, had received his final instructions from the General and left for Washington. Later, he wondered whether some strange power was not operating to prevent the great crusader's dream from coming true. For as the recent months had sped by, the chief participants in the General's last campaign had passed on almost in a timed cycle of death.

There was Joseph W. Byrns, Speaker of the House, who had signed the aircraft probe subpoenas; Senator Robinson, determined to re-establish Mitchell; Dern, the Secretary of War, who lived long enough to regret some of his actions in the Air controversy; Sirovich, found dead in his bathtub; Senator Lundeen, supporter of a vigorous air policy, victim of the worst airplane disaster in years.

The dying General's warning of personal danger also was to be remembered by the investigator when he returned to his apartment one evening from Washington whither he had flown with all records of the investigation.

The fact-finder was dragged out of his burning room after a violent explosion in the fireplace which sent him to the hospital and kept him in bandages for months. Looking into foreign influences in the aircraft industry was truly a job which could not have been described as monotonous.

The loneliness and weariness of the trail of yellowed documents of evidence, its pitfalls and disappointments, had worn the investigator down to a deep pitch of despondency when the news reached him that the greatest man he had ever known was gone. Billy Mitchell was no more!

The investigator, in need of companionship, and consolation, sought out his friend Martin, the old inventor, who had grasped the General's hand before the end, when the clasp held more words than the lips.

"He must have gone in the morning, after I saw him," the inventor tried to explain. "He was saying something about Generals in peace; something about wars being won by Generals who are active and vigilant in peace. He said he had been tried—but his trial was not over. After he was gone, he would be still on trial, he said, 'For how long, how long?' he kept asking. I remember, particularly, certain of his words, when he couldn't say much, and I looked at him hard, but he nodded as if to tell me he knew—he knew what he was talking about. I didn't catch all of what he said—something about 'flying all over the world and possibly beyond our world into interstellar space.' "

"He wrote that," the investigator interrupted. "He left that message to his children in his last book. He told them they would live to see tremendous things in the sky—that there was no space, really."

"But he kept talking about that trial," Martin said, clearing his voice, his face turned away. "He wanted to know how long it was going to last, and I told him..."

"Yes, yes. I understand," the investigator said, quietly. "What did you tell him?"

"I told him—I told him the jury was in and that the American people had found him—not guilty."

THE END

Printed in Great Britain
by Amazon

19813698R00103